To Be
Human

August 1, 2016
   600
   5½" x 8½"
Perfectbound paperback
Interiors: RR Donnelley
   240 pages
   50# Domtar Earthchoice, 400 ppi
   1/c black throughout
covers: RR Donnelley
   10 pt. C1S
   4/c process
   matte lamination

Books by J. Krishnamurti

To Be
Human

J. KRISHNAMURTI

Edited by David Skitt

SHAMBHALA
Boulder
2000

SHAMBHALA PUBLICATIONS, INC.
4720 Walnut Street
Boulder, Colorado 80301
www.shambhala.com

Edited by David Skitt

17   16   15   14   13   12   11   10   9
Printed in the United States of America

For information about Foundations, Schools, and Study Centers, please write to:

Krishnamurti Foundation Trust
Brockwood Park
Bramdean, Hampshire SO24 0LQ
England
kft@brockwood.org.uk

or

Krishnamurti Foundation of America
P.O. Box 1560
Ojai, CA 93024-1560
U.S.A.
kfa@kfa.org
www.kfa.org

Distributed in the United States by Penguin Random House LLC and in Canada by Random House of Canada Ltd

Library of Congress Cataloging-in-Publication Data
Krishnamurti, J. (Jiddu), 1895–1986
To be human / J. Krishnamurti ; edited by David Skitt.—1st ed.
p.   cm.
ISBN 978-1-57062-596-1 (paper)
1. Human beings.   I. Skitt, David.   II. Title.
B5134.K753 T6   2000
128—dc21
00-041994

Don't accept anything the speaker is saying. Test it out for yourself.

—

You must become liberated not because of me but in spite of me.

—

If you really faced the world as it is, and tackled it, you would find it something infinitely greater than any philosophy, greater than any book in the world, greater than any teaching, greater than any teacher.

—J. KRISHNAMURTI

Contents

————

PART II
Words and Meanings

PART III
Action through Inaction

EDITOR'S INTRODUCTION
Philosophy without Boundaries

———

W HAT WOULD IT MEAN to talk about "a rebirth of philosophy"? It would have to mean something like restoring its relevance to the way that you and I live our everyday lives. It would also presuppose that the philosophy be expressed in words that are sufficiently intelligible to us, which in turn would require a passionate concern by the philosopher to communicate his or her insights as clearly and widely as possible.

Candidates without these qualifications need not apply.

A rebirth of philosophy might also be seen to demand that the word *philosophy* be used in its original, true sense—the love of wisdom, a word one has only to say to realize how little we use it, though it still appears, one hopes not too precariously, in the *Concise Oxford English Dictionary*. And how is *wisdom* defined? The 1995 version is "experience and knowledge together with the power of applying them critically." In a previous edition it was "the intelligent application of knowledge."

These definitions come surprisingly close to the heart of what Krishnamurti is talking about—let us call it, for the moment, his "philosophy." Again and again he points to the crucial importance of applying knowledge and experience where they have their place and of not applying them where they do not, where life demands that we look and act anew. This turns out not to be as simple as it sounds. It has deep implications for the way we see and act, whether personally, socially, or politically. These implications and what prevents the human mind from performing well and harmoniously in both areas, the known and the unknown, are matters Krishnamurti tirelessly explores.

Krishnamurti is also a philosopher in the original sense in renewing the age-long debate on the nature of truth, which will no doubt seem to some of us hopelessly old-fashioned and naive and to others of us long overdue. But in general, and despite Pontius Pilate's ever-skeptical "What is truth?" we all have to be concerned about what is true and what is not over a whole range of practical issues, whether the rights and wrongs of personal relationships or of disputes between nations. Like it or not, the notion of truth gate-crashes its way into our lives. It is also significant that when some years ago a mainstream publisher conducted a survey of general readers to discover what fundamental issues interested them most, it was truth that headed the list.

Again, it is clear that at least part of the huge public fascination in the United States with the televised O. J. Simpson trial was due to the opportunity it offered viewers to weigh evidence and determine the truth for themselves. One of the most striking incidents occurred when the prosecution showed a video to demonstrate the scientific rigor with which a forensic scientist had collected a bloodstain from a pavement. When the video ended, the defense immediately insisted it be reshown and argued that it proved precisely the opposite—the scientist's incompetence. Enough to baffle any jury, what this incident revealed beyond all doubt was the crucial problem of human perception—we don't necessarily see what is "true" in the same way. Sometimes this doesn't matter and can be enriching. Sometimes we find it disturbing and annoying. On other occasions it can lead to human beings' exterminating huge numbers of their own species.

So here again one can argue that by exploring the issue of truth, Krishnamurti is going back to the roots of philosophy. In the way he does it, however, he shatters the strongly entrenched academic frontiers drawn in our time between the provinces of philosophy, psychology, science, and religion. Krishnamurti will raise any issue, from any area of human activity, which he considers relevant to the way we see ourselves, others, life, and the universe. One doesn't have to share his views to feel a refreshing sense of freedom about that.*

While Krishnamurti often specifically rejected for himself the term *philosopher*, he also expressed respect for the original meaning of *philosophy* as "the love of truth and wisdom in one's daily life now"—this being the sense in which the term is used in the title of this introduction. Why did he reject the current usage? Perhaps there is a clue in a talk he gave a few years before his death in 1986. He had put the question to his audience: "What is beyond all time, what is the source, the origin of all creation?" Many of us would find this an arresting question, though some of us would dismiss it out of hand as metaphysical. What was his answer? The audience waited expectantly. He did not give one. Instead, he discussed the nature of a mind that would be capable of going into such a question.

In this age of experts, this is not something that we are used to. If we go to a philosophy lecture on the nature of reality or listen to a TV discussion on the mind as computer, we expect explanations and answers. We do not expect to hear a discourse on the quality of mind we need to explore these issues, particularly if we have had a lot of formal and possibly expensive education. We might feel let down, perhaps affronted.

Less demandingly, contemporary philosophers have usually seen it as their role to expound their analysis of language, their theories, their new concepts. They do not suggest to their students that there is first of all a state of mind in which these topics need to be approached. But this is precisely what Krishnamurti

---

*It is interesting in this regard to note the conclusion to the article on philosophy in the *Macmillan Encyclopedia of Philosophy*, 1974 edition. John Passmore writes: "There is room within philosophy for an immense variety of types of investigation, some minute and some highly generalized. Nor is it a matter of any importance if a philosopher, in trying to solve a particular problem, passes outside the boundaries of philosophy altogether. In the end, it is problems, not the divisions between subjects, that are crucial."

repeatedly suggests.* So one's first reaction may be to find this condescending and even arrogant. But look again at the quotations preceding the table of contents (p. v). The first asserts the ability of the listener to test and challenge the validity of what Krishnamurti says; the second warns against giving any authority, or any significance at all, to his person; while the third declares life to be the supreme teacher for all of us. Note that all three statements express deep respect for the actual and potential abilities of human beings in general, not just of an elite.

—

A key feature of Krishnamurti's philosophy is his insistence that it be "tested out," "doubted," "questioned," even "torn to pieces." Essentially this means testing the truth of the propositions he puts to us against our everyday experience. If one does not do so, he argues, we are left with the "ashes of words." There may well be difficulties, however, in the way of such testing. The human tendency to worship someone, to idolize political leaders and religious saviors, to cling emotionally to beliefs, to "have faith" is obvious, as is the widespread confusion and strife it causes. As the psychologist Erich Fromm, among others, has convincingly argued, God, religious dignitaries, and even political dictators easily become parental figures, the unconditionally loving and masterful mother or father we never had. Fromm also saw in this tendency a masochistic submission to authority, a view borne out by the recent testimony on BBC radio of a Russian who, imprisoned for fifteen years in a Siberian gulag for anti-Soviet remarks, described how he clutched a doorpost and wept on the death of

---

*This is not entirely at odds with a contemporary, academic definition of philosophy. The 1994 edition of the *Oxford Dictionary of Philosophy* states as a general principle that "in philosophy, the concepts with which we approach the world themselves become the topic of enquiry." But it goes on to add, "At different times there has been more or less optimism about the possibility of a pure or 'first' philosophy, taking an *a priori* standpoint from which other intellectual practices can be impartially assessed and subjected to logical evaluation and correction. The late 20th-century spirit of the subject is hostile to any such possibility, and prefers to see philosophical reflection as continuous with the best practice of any field of intellectual enquiry."

Stalin. It was several years, he said, before it dawned on him that Stalin was why he was there.

So it is hardly surprising that in some people's eyes, an aura of World Teacher or Messiah always clung to Krishnamurti, despite everything he said to nullify such an image in their minds.

> If you really faced the world as it is, and tackled it, you would find it something infinitely greater than any philosophy, greater than any book in the world, greater than any teaching, greater than any teacher.

> Whether I am the World Teacher or the Messiah or something else is surely not important. If it is important to you then you will miss the truth of what I am saying because you will judge by the label—and the label is so flimsy. Somebody will say that I am the Messiah and somebody else will say that I am not and then where are you? What is important is to find out whether what I say is the truth by examining it and finding out whether it can be worked out in daily life.

> The speaker is speaking for himself, not for anybody else. He may be deceiving himself, he may be trying to pretend to be something or other. He may be, you don't know. So have a great deal of scepticism, doubt, question.

Yet for many people the mystique lingered, and for some seemed all-important. It is true that both the person and his life were by any conventional standard extraordinary. His presence was found by many people to convey a deep stillness, energy, and vitality, and for many, but not all, of those closest to him, unconditional love. But how did people then handle or interpret their reactions to this unintended charisma? How much was autosuggestion or excitement at being close to someone exceptional? Did one have a kind of self-induced "high," possibly at odds with listening to what he was saying? If you regard someone as "the World Teacher" with all the emotional glow that can bring, you may fear to lose that glow and to be disloyal by doubting and questioning, even when constantly urged by him to do so. Late in his life, Krishnamurti said that those very close to him generally did not understand what he was talking about—"It becomes more of a personal worship, a personal sense of being close together." There is plenty of evidence that nearness to a person one holds in awe can wreak havoc with one's critical faculty.

Problems in this regard can also exist for people who never met or heard Krishnamurti in person. As he said himself, his style is "emphatic." His use of the word *obviously* often follows propositions one may not find obvious at all. This may be deliberately provocative, to jolt listeners out of their usual complacency. Certainly he made many statements that have an authoritative, take-it-or-leave-it ring about them. And to the extent that one is longing for certainty, one may swallow these uncritically—with later mental indigestion. Always, as the following example shows, there is a need to look carefully at the context.

"The new mind comes into being and explodes." A remark like this can have a heady, almost seductive quality, a sense of something that is boundless and fulfilling. The thought arises: it would be great to have that. But this may easily cause one to skim lightly over what comes next: "And that is hard, arduous work. It requires constant watching." And there follows a very dense and demanding account of what such watching entails (see the talk at Bombay on March 12, 1961).

In other words, when reading Krishnamurti, it is tempting to get carried away by one's pleasant imagining of the "end result"— which is actually, he would warn, merely a blinkered projection of one's present, limited experience. But this may feel much more agreeable than plumbing objectively the depths of that experience—"watching" it—for everything that one needs to learn from it.

Other difficulties arise from the inherent failure of language to convey precisely notions that we nonetheless universally regard as significant. Such concepts as intelligence and the self spring to mind. Though Krishnamurti's vocabulary is simple, it is by no means easy to understand either on a first or later reading. As he himself said, "You have to learn my vocabulary, the meaning behind the words." To some extent this reflects the difficulty that all psychologists and philosophers have in describing the complex and subtle ways in which our minds function, or fail to. Those who feel they have something new to say usually coin and define a set of new concepts. Krishnamurti deliberately rejected this but made it clear in the 1930s that he would be using language in a special way. He also cautioned his listeners about the limitations inherent in language.

> Words are only of value if they convey the true significance of the ideas behind the words. . . . You cannot describe something which is indescribable in words. But words must be used, as a painter uses paint on a canvas to convey the significance of his vision. But if you are merely caught in the technique of painting, then you will not catch the full significance of the idea which the painter wishes to convey. In all my talks, I am giving a new interpretation to words. It will be very difficult therefore for you to understand, if you are merely caught in the words. You must go beyond the words, and strive to catch the significance which I give to those words, and not just give to them your own convenient meaning.

> As the majority of people have a fixed habit of thought, and translate every new idea put before them into that habit of thought, naturally it is very difficult for me to explain something new in old words. Yet I must use ordinary words. I cannot invent a new language, but I can give a new interpretation to the words that I am using. If you use words as a bridge, so that understanding is established, then words have a very definite value: but if you allow yourself to become entangled in words, then words have no value.

Repeatedly Krishnamurti also makes the point that "the word is not the thing." Words are not their referents. This seems simple enough for external objects. The word *table* is not the table itself. And in everyday usage, we can all assume that "what a table is" is not a problem. But for psychological states and processes, the situation is more complex. For example, while we may be able to give the dictionary definition of *boredom* and use the word fluently in a discussion, this needs to be clearly distinguished from a real understanding of "what boredom is," which can be derived only from actual experience of the state and from exploring its psychological implications to the full.

We know that the same word—*love* is a prime example—may be used glibly, superficially, or as a deep pointer to the state itself, and one of the great problems of communication stressed by Krishnamurti is whether the "communicators"—say, two people talking together—share the same deep concern for what they are discussing. If they are both deeply concerned about something and deeply concerned to communicate it, the right words will come. But a barrier to communication arises when words are used emotively by one party and are heard as such, so that they have a strong, agitating, neurological impact. They cease then to be pointers, fall out of their natural role, and seem, by a kind of conjuring trick, to become that which they point to. Politically, terms like *national sovereignty* and *freedom* are good examples of words that get easily perverted in this way and are used to control and manipulate. But it isn't just politicians who use words in this way. We all need, Krishnamurti argues, to be wary of words and to dig behind them.

The second part of this book, called "Words and Meanings," therefore gives a number of examples of the "old" words to which, as Krishnamurti said, he gave "new" meanings. Unless the first-time reader is aware of such renovation, many of his statements may puzzle and lack clarity. His unusual use of language is also illustrated by a number of passages on words in general.

—

The answering of questions—or, better, the putting to ourselves of really important questions—and the solving of problems depend, in Krishnamurti's view, on the quality of our observation, both inward and outward. Put simply, just as scientists have to look to the quality of the apparatus with which they observe subatomic particles, we all need to be concerned—and constantly so—with the quality and clarity of our minds. Such concern is not just the mental equivalent of half an hour's jogging a day. It needs to be as constant as possible, free from any objective, and demands a passionate concern with clarity for clarity's sake.

Is this possible? We know that when we have an ambition, we can give unbounded energy to it. François Mitterand once explained how to become the president of France—"A president is twenty years in the making. You have to give up everything for it, be concerned about it from the time you put your socks on until you go to bed." So it depends where you put your energy. Mitterand's statement contrasts—piquantly—with Krishnamurti's observation, "Apparently few have that deep passion which dedicates itself to the understanding of the whole process of living, rather than giving their whole energy to fragmentary activity."

——

Krishnamurti often said that he could only "point to the door." We, if we so wish, have to get up and open it. And we must feel absolutely free to do this or not to do this. So, if the door is to swing open, what has to be done? And how can Krishnamurti possibly claim, as he does, that he is not proposing any system, method, or practice and is in no way setting himself up as an authority?

One way of answering these necessary questions is to start with the way we look, visually, at the world around us. Some present-day psychologists and neuroscientists have argued that perception of visual stimuli can be thought of as a search for the best interpretation of sensory information, and that from a cognitive viewpoint, a perceived object is a hypothesis suggested by the sensory data. So they see perception not as a process of passive sensing of such data, but as an active one of observing and testing the hypotheses they suggest in order to find the one that is most consistent with the sensory data.

This kind of observing and hypothesis-testing operates constantly in science, where subsequent confirmation of the results is the basis for determining what is scientifically true. Although without the rigor of science and its concern to duplicate results, the same basic process is used more simply by all of us in everyday situations. "I'll see if taking the car rather than the train will get me to work quicker." "Change the plug and see if the lamp will work." "If I offer to do overtime now, I'll see if I can get leave in July." "Maybe relations with my unhelpful colleague will improve if I buy him a drink." This is a natural and essential process that we all need to use to live our daily lives reasonably effectively. So one way of approaching Krishnamurti is to see him as offering us hypotheses about the workings of the human mind that it is open to each of us to test.

What is proposed here is something that is as transnational and cross-cultural, and as universal in its application, as science, but operating in a very different field—the way we handle everyday living. It should not be seen as needing to invoke the support of science, although it can be regarded as "science-friendly." For in whatever society and culture human beings find themselves, whatever their prevailing religious and political beliefs, they all have to make and test hypotheses or assumptions about reality. It is this natural ability that Krishnamurti sees as crucial, as supreme, calling on us to use and to deepen it, asking us to consider which of our assumptions are the most important to explore and test.

—

Is there, according to Krishnamurti, a specific problem that human beings have in observing what is going on within them and around them? What prevents the clarity and objectivity that life demands if we are not to waste much of it in conflict and delusion? Is there one proposition in particular in this area that he invites us to test?

In almost every talk he gave, Krishnamurti used the phrase "the observer is the observed" and spoke of "observing without the observer." It may well be that the understanding of these propositions, and of others that he makes, is not possible without at least some psychological experimentation. Testing them is necessary for them to become fully meaningful, and the third part of this book contains passages in which Krishnamurti points to ways of carrying out such testing. Perhaps an attempt at summarizing these propositions here may be useful.

In peak—call them phase one—experiences, such as strong anger or great delight, we do not have any sense of separation from what we are experiencing. I do not weigh up my anger, resolve not to give way to it in future, or find reasons for justifying it. In the case of delight, I do not start thinking about the next opportunity for experiencing it. In both cases I am *at one with* the sensation. But as this peak experience subsides, a phase two, *a duality*, a separation, a split of that kind does occur, and is expressed in such thoughts as "I should not have lost my temper" or "So-and-so deserved it," and so on. In the case of unpleasant experiences, such as loneliness, there can also be a tactic of escape, such as switching on the radio, having a drink, phoning someone, thus suppressing the unpleasantness and so strengthening one's capacity to reexperience it; while after a peak experience of pleasure, there is usually a mulling over, a "chewing the cud," an "addiction" to its repetition.

What happens here—in phase two—Krishnamurti sees as a conflictual split in the psyche, the emergence of an imaginary "observer" who separates himself or herself from what was being experienced. This rift Krishnamurti sees as a source of endless conflict both within oneself, with others, and indeed collectively among nations. What can be done? He answers, "Nothing." He simply proposes that when these separative thoughts and images arise, one should "stay with" them. This signifies not escaping, not condemning or justifying, not seeking to change or get rid of them, but "holding them like a baby" with care, affection, and curiosity. This nonjudgmental monitoring, or "choiceless awareness" in Krishnamurti's phrase, also implies ceasing mentally to name the sensation being experienced, since such naming carries a heavy charge from our past experiences of it that conditions our present experience.

In this choiceless awareness or "observing without the observer," the thoughts and images subside, like water that has been stirred and muddied returning to a state of clear stillness. This stillness is, however, energizing. In it there can arise insights into the true significance, the origin, workings, and limitation of the thoughts and images experienced: "If the mind is aware of its limitation without condemnation, without justification, if it is purely aware of its limitation, then you will find there comes a freedom from that limitation. And in that freedom, truth is realized."

The present writer is under no illusions about his brief summary's doing justice to this crucial theme, which runs through all Krishnamurti's work and has implications for the way we see not only ourselves but also others and life in general. Still, if it prompts a reader to turn to the many passages in Krishnamurti on this subject, and to test them against everyday experience, it will have served its purpose.

This is perhaps a good place to mention that Krishnamurti often referred to this kind of exploration as an activity needing a "desirable seriousness which also has its own humor." Of observing without the observer, he said: "This cannot be taught by another; it comes through your observation of yourself, watching all the time. You know, it's great fun if you don't condemn or justify but watch 'what is.'" And he described the learning involved as follows: "Learning is fun. To see new things is great fun. It gives you tremendous energy if you make a great discovery for yourself—not if someone else discovers it and tells you about it, then it's second-hand. When you are learning, it is fun to see something totally new, like discovering a new insect, a new species. To discover how my mind is working, to see all the nuances, the subtleties, to learn about it is fun."

—

Is Krishnamurti saying something new?

As far as Eastern sources are concerned, there has been clear recognition of the importance of Krishnamurti's works by Buddhist authorities such as the Dalai Lama and Walpola Rahula, the author of the article on the Buddha in the *Encyclopaedia Britannica.* A similar recognition has been expressed by Vedanta scholars such as Venkatesananda.

The Western reaction has been more mixed. His works are on the syllabus of more than two hundred American universities and colleges, and he has been the subject of Ph.D. theses in England, France, and Germany. Apart from educational theory—as a recent book, *Reflections on the Self,* edited by Raymond Martin, professor of philosophy at Maryland University, has shown—it is clear that personal identity is the area where classical and contemporary Western philosophy overlaps most of all with Krishnamurti's work. Also, as Martin points out, Krishnamurti can be said to revive the use of the Socratic question. And in the purely British tradition, there is a debate that runs from Berkeley and Hume through F. H. Bradley, Bernard Williams, and Derek Parfit on problems of the self that are also of concern to Krishnamurti.

But there are very radical differences of both expression and approach. For although Krishnamurti wrote several books, his preferred medium of expression was the spoken word rather than the more formal structure of the book, reflecting the unfolding and open-endedness of life, the moving picture rather than the still. Even more radically, he urged his listeners to abandon all authority, including that of one's own experience, when observing oneself, others, and life. His own answer to the question "Is there anything new in your teaching?" illustrates this clearly.

To find out for yourself is much more important than my asserting "yes" or "no." It is your problem, not my problem. To me all this is totally new because it has to be discovered from moment to moment. It cannot be stored up after discovery; it is not something to be experienced and then retained as memory—which would be putting new wine in old bottles. It must be discovered as one lives from day to day, and it is new to the person who discovers it. But you are always comparing what is being said with what has been said by some saint or by Shankara, Buddha, or Christ. You say, "All these people have said this before, and you are giving it another twist, a modern expression." So naturally it is then nothing new to you. It is only when you have ceased to compare, so that your mind is alone, clear, no longer influenced, controlled, compelled, either by modern psychology or by the ancient sanctions and edicts, that you will find out whether or not there is something new, everlasting. But that requires vigor, not indolence. It demands a drastic cutting away of all the things that one has read or been told about truth or God.

A fundamental objection by academic philosophers and psychologists to this passage is that it relies too much on inner observation and on "private" sensations. The inaccessibility of such observation and sensations to others is invoked to dismiss this whole area as inherently subjective and not amenable to any process of verification that could be called objective or scientific. It is therefore ruled out as a legitimate area of inquiry.

Yet there is something about such a judgment that smacks of a guillotined debate. The charge of subjectivity notwithstanding, there are counterarguments to it. First of all, there is the case for a commonsense view. For all of us, the way we see ourselves and others, the variety and quality of our sensations, are hugely important for the way we experience our lives. *Essentially, they are what being alive means.* It would also become very difficult for human beings to function at all unless we had some confidence in our self-exploration and our ability to see the truth of at least some of the situations we encounter. Without some consensus on what is true, human relationships and society would disintegrate.

The question then is: can one human being, from his or her experience, throw fresh light on the quality of mind we all need— say, clarity—and point to what fundamentally limits it? Krishnamurti's response to this in his own case is twofold: First, doubt, question, challenge what I am saying. Second, test what I say in practice. The whole issue is tossed back into the lap of each of us. We need to be skeptical, he says, and to find out the answer to this for ourselves.

———

Krishnamurti's literary legacy in the form of talks, discussions, and writings has been estimated to equal the contents of four hundred average-sized books. Of this total material, some fifty or so major books have been compiled and translated into many of the world's languages. Also, in the course of his long life, he may have engaged in serious debate with more people in personal interviews than anyone has ever done. Many of these conversations went unrecorded.

In light of this vast output, known and unknown, the task of putting together a short collection of texts serving as an introduction to his work is formidable, if not foolhardy. Also, whatever texts one chooses will invalidate the very notion of an introduction. But before the would-be compiler despairs, a handrail of sorts presents itself. In 1980, Krishnamurti wrote, on request, a one-page summary of his work, which he himself referred to as the "core" of his teaching.

The present book therefore starts with this summary and follows it with a selection of passages of an amplifying kind. So far, so good, one might think. This should provide a neat and tidy nutshell. In a way it does—but it also calls immediately for some qualification.

The qualification arises because any prolonged study of Krishnamurti's "teaching"—or "whatever it is," as he himself once put it—confronts one with a mind whose nature is constantly unfolding and deepening, always dynamic and never static. This nature follows in part from his great emphasis on the new and unknown in life as vital and enhancing aspects of human existence: "Life is the unknown, as death is the unknown, as truth is the unknown." There is something new, therefore, in every moment of being. The challenge is to see it.

For Krishnamurti, that which is new, unknown, unpredictable in life needs to be met with a movement of total attention that is not conditioned by past experience—although the intelligence that he sees operating in attention will know when to draw upon that experience.

The consequence of this view of life as creative learning, as pristinely new, is that a reader hoping to find in it a set of conclusions about the human condition, with something of the comforting fixity of the Great Pyramid, will be disappointed. What he or she will find is a number of statements about the way we perceive life, ourselves, and others, which, if tested by us and found to be true, will, he argues, open the door to an ongoing awareness of the "immensity" of life. First-time readers should be cautioned again, however, that Krishnamurti's style, when making these testable statements, while by definition not dogmatic, can certainly be emphatic.

There is another way in which a book of introductory texts may be said to sit uneasily with what he is talking about. His testable statements are clearly inseparable from learning about oneself, about others, about life as a whole. Now, the way we do that is usually much more haphazard than the steady perusal of a printed text. Life springs surprises on us, gives lessons at its own pace and frequency, not ours. Much of the attraction of a book is that its structure seems to reassuringly impose order on a mercurial world. Also, with a book, we are in charge, in the sense that we pick it up, put it down, dip into it at will. *We* are in control. Of the book, yes—but hardly of life. However, for some readers at least, the unexpectedness of Krishnamurti may dispel any cramping sense of bookish order.

—

The last part of this book contains a series of extracts that describe three simple actions: "Staying with 'What Is,' " "Asking but Not Answering Fundamental Questions," and "The Beauty of Not Knowing." One could also call them "inactions from which actions spring." They are given as examples only, not as an authoritative guide. All three can be seen as natural human abilities, not anything one would call a newly minted method or technique. To some extent we already use these abilities, indeed have to. We know at the time of bereavement that it is healthy and right to embrace, to stay with, one's grief, rather than to escape from and suppress it. The importance of "knowing when you do not know" is something that many of us have heard from a school or university teacher. And finding a solution after "sleeping on" a problem is something all of us have done at one time or another.

What Krishnamurti is suggesting here, therefore, can in a way be seen as very simple—a wider and deeper application of natural faculties of the mind. However, this is not for him just a matter of useful enhancement, but an urgent and deep need, something life requires of us. It is neglect of these faculties that causes conflict and distress, and before they can flourish, we need to be aware of and understand the reasons for that neglect.

The concluding pages of the book contain a number of quotations on issues that come up frequently in discussions of Krishnamurti's work.

Finally, how far one is willing to test what Krishnamurti says will depend on whether one feels that Albert Speer's problem of "seeing only what one wants to see and knowing only what one wants to know" is not just a problem for a minister of the Third Reich but entangles all of us. Not all blinkered perception is as searingly inhuman as Speer's. But many of us experience conflict and confusion with others because we do not see, or do not want to see, the same things in the same way. And so a great deal of human life and energy are lost in painful and destructive friction, whether in personal relationships or among nations. In the end, exploring the issues Krishnamurti raises will hinge on whether one feels that to understand oneself and others and life in general, and to be passionate about that, is what life demands of us most of all, is the essence of being human.

PART I

The Core
of the
Teaching

What follows is in Krishnamurti's words
unless otherwise indicated.

Listening

—

I HOPE YOU WILL have the patience to listen to this. Communication is anyhow very difficult because words have definite
meanings; consciously, we accept certain definitions and try to
translate what we hear according to those definitions. But if we
begin to define every word . . . and leave it at that, communication will be at the conscious level. It seems to me that what we
are discussing is not merely to be understood at the conscious
level, but also to be absorbed—if I may put it that way—
unconsciously, deep down, without the formulation of definition.
It is far more important to listen with the depth of one's whole
being, than to indulge in merely superficial explanations. If we
can listen in that way, with the totality of one's being, that very
listening is an act of meditation.

You have to listen without any effort, without any struggle.
It is a very difficult problem to listen with the totality of one's
being—that is, when the mind not only hears the words, but is
capable of going beyond the words. The mere judgment of a
conscious mind is not the discovery or the understanding of truth.
The conscious mind can never find that which is real. All that
it can do is to choose, judge, weigh, compare. But comparison,
judgment, or identification is not the uncovering of truth. That is
why it is very important to know how to listen. When you read a
book, you might translate what you read according to your partic-

ular tendency, knowledge, or idiosyncrasy, and so miss the whole content of what the author wants to convey; but to understand, to discover, you have to listen without the resistance of the conscious mind which wants to debate, discuss, analyze. Debating, discussing, analyzing is a hindrance when we are dealing with matters which require not mere verbal definition and superficial understanding, but understanding at a much deeper, more fundamental level. Such understanding, the understanding of truth, depends upon how one listens.

—

Can one listen without any conclusion, without any comparison or judgment, just listen, as you would listen to music, to something which you really feel you love? Then you listen not only with your mind, your intellect, but you also listen with your heart, you listen with care, objectively, sanely, you listen with attention to find out.

—

I think there is an art of listening, which is to listen completely without any motive, because a motive in listening is a distraction. If you can listen with complete attention, then there is no resistance, either to your own thoughts or to what is being said— which does not mean you will be mesmerized by words. But it is only the very silent, quiet mind that finds out what is true, not a mind which is furiously active, thinking, resisting.

—

I do not know if you have ever tried this. That is, to listen to the words and to find out the truth of any statement that is made by the speaker, not only intellectually, not only with considerable doubt, but also to listen without any resistance—which does not mean accepting, but to listen so profoundly, with great attention, so that the very act of listening brings about a total breaking-down of the pattern of the brain.

The Core of the Teaching

THE CORE OF KRISHNAMURTI'S teaching is contained in
the statement he made in 1929 when he said: "Truth is a
pathless land."* Man cannot come to it through any organization,
through any creed, through any dogma, priest, or ritual, nor
through any philosophical knowledge or psychological technique. He has to find it through the mirror of relationship,
through the understanding of the contents of his own mind,
through observation and not through intellectual analysis or in-
trospective dissection. Man has built in himself images as a fence
of security—religious, political, personal. These manifest as symbols, ideas, beliefs. The burden of these images dominates man's
thinking, his relationships, and his daily life. These images are
the causes of our problems, for they divide man from man. His
perception of life is shaped by the concepts already established
in his mind. The content of his consciousness is his entire existence. This content is common to all humanity. The individuality
is the name, the form, and superficial culture he acquires from
tradition and environment. The uniqueness of man does not lie in
the superficial but in complete freedom from the content of his

*This summary was originally written by Krishnamurti himself on October 21,
1980, for "Krishnamurti: The Years of Fulfilment" by Mary Lutyens, published
by John Murray Ltd in 1983. On a later rereading, Krishnamurti added a few
sentences, which are included here.

consciousness, which is common to all mankind. So he is not an individual.

Freedom is not a reaction. Freedom is not choice. It is man's pretense that because he has choice, he is free. Freedom is pure observation without direction, without fear of punishment and reward. Freedom is without motive; freedom is not at the end of the evolution of man but lies in the first step of his existence. In observation one begins to discover the lack of freedom. Freedom is found in the choiceless awareness of our daily existence and activity. Thought is time. Thought is born of experience and knowledge, which are inseparable from time and the past. Time is the psychological enemy of man. Our action is based on knowledge and therefore time, so man is always a slave to the past. Thought is ever-limited, and so we live in constant conflict and struggle. There is no psychological evolution. When man becomes aware of the movement of his own thoughts, he will see the division between the thinker and the thought, the observer and the observed, the experiencer and the experience. He will discover that this division is an illusion. Then only is there pure observation, which is insight without any shadow of the past or of time. This timeless insight brings about a deep radical mutation in the mind.

Total negation is the essence of the positive. When there is negation of all those things that thought has brought about psychologically, only then is there love, which is compassion and intelligence.

Truth Is a Pathless Land

To me there is no path to truth. Truth is not to be understood through any system, through any path. A path implies a goal, a static end, and therefore a conditioning of the mind and heart by that end, which necessarily demands discipline, control, and acquisitiveness. This discipline, this control becomes a burden. It robs you of freedom and conditions your action in daily life.

—

Truth is something to be understood, to be discovered in every action, in every thought, in every feeling, however trivial, however transient. Truth is something to be looked at, to be listened to—to what your husband says, or what your wife says, or what the gardener says, what your friends say, or what your own thinking is. To discover the truth of what you think—because your thoughts may be false or your thoughts may be conditioned—to discover that your thought is conditioned is truth. To discover that your thought is limited is truth. That very discovery sets your mind free from limitation.

If I discover that I am greedy—discover it, not be told by you that I am greedy—that very discovery is truth, that very truth has an action upon my greed. Truth is not something which is gathered, accumulated, stored up, upon which you can rely as a guide.

If you do, it is only another form of the same thing, another form of possession. It is very difficult for the mind not to acquire, not to store. When you realize this, you will find out what an extraordinary thing truth is.

—

The fact is that truth is life and life has no permanency. Life has to be discovered from moment to moment, from day to day. It has to be discovered. It cannot be taken for granted. If you take it for granted that you know life, then you are not living. Three meals a day, clothing, shelter, sex, your job, your amusement, and your thinking process—that dull, repetitive process is not life.

Life is something to be discovered. And you cannot discover it if you have not lost, put aside the things that you have found. Do experiment with what I am saying. Put aside your philosophies, your religions, your customs, your racial taboos, and all the rest of it. For they are not life. If you are caught in those things, you will never discover life.

A man who says he knows is already dead. But the man who thinks "I don't know," who is discovering, finding out, who is not seeking an end, not thinking in terms of arriving or becoming—such a man is living, and that living is truth.

Is There Such a Thing as Truth Apart from Personal Opinion?

———

QUESTIONER: There is a prevalent assumption these days that everything is relative and a matter of personal opinion, that there is no such thing as truth or fact independent of personal perception. What is an intelligent response to this belief?

KRISHNAMURTI: Is it that we are all so terribly personal? What I see, what you see, is the only truth? My opinion and your opinion are the only facts we have? That is what the question implies, that everything is relative. So goodness is relative, evil is relative, love is relative. And as everything is relative—that is, not whole, complete truth—then our action, our affection in personal relationship is relative, and can be ended whenever we like, whenever it doesn't please us, and so on. That is the implication of this question.

Now is there—we are both of us investigating, please, I am not telling you—such a thing as truth, apart from personal opinion, personal belief, personal perception? This question has been asked by the ancient Greeks and Hindus, and by the Buddhists. And it is one of the strange facts about the Eastern religions that doubt was encouraged. To doubt, to question. And in Western religions, this is rather put down. If you doubt, it is called heresy. So apart from personal opinions, perceptions, experiences, which are always relative, one must find out for oneself whether there is a perception, a seeing, which is absolute and not relative truth.

Now how are you going to find out? If we say that personal opinion, personal perception, is relative, and there is no such thing as absolute truth, then truth is relative. And our behavior, our conduct, our way of life will accordingly be relative, casual, not complete, not whole, therefore fragmentary. And we are trying to find out if there is such a thing as truth that is not just personal opinion, personal perception.

If this question is put to you, how would you find out if there is truth that is absolute, complete, which is not just relative and always changing with the climate of personal opinion? How does your mind, the intellect, or thought find out? Does this interest you? Because here you are inquiring into something that demands a great deal of investigation, of action in daily life, a sense of putting aside that which is false. That is the only way to proceed. For if we have an illusion, a fantasy, an image, a romantic concept of truth, or of love or whatever, those are the very barriers that prevent us from moving further.

Can one honestly investigate an illusion? Does the mind live in illusion? Or do we have illusions about everything, about people, about nations, about religion, about God? How do illusions come into being? How does one have an illusion, what is the root of it? What do we mean by the word *illusion*? It comes from the Latin, *ludere*, which means "to play." So the root meaning is to play, to play with something that is not actual. The actual is what is happening, what is actually taking place, whether it is called good, bad, or indifferent. And when one is incapable of facing what is actually taking place in oneself, then to escape from that is to create illusion.

Please don't agree, I am just exploring this, we are exploring together.

So if one is unwilling or afraid to face, or wants to avoid, what is actually going on, that very avoidance creates an illusion, a fantasy, a romantic movement away from "what is." Can we accept that as the meaning of the word *illusion*, moving away from "what is," and go on from there? Please don't agree with me; see this as a fact.

The next question is: can we avoid this movement, this escape from actuality? So then we ask, what is the actual? The actual is that which is happening, the actual responses, ideas, the actual belief, the actual opinion you have. And to face that is not to create illusion. Have we gone this far in our investigation? Because otherwise you can't go further.

So as long as there are illusions, opinions, perceptions, based on the avoidance of "what is," these must be relative—there must be relativeness. This is bound to be so when there is a movement away from the fact, from what is happening, from "what is." In understanding "what is," it is not your personal opinion, not your personal perception that judges "what is," but actual observation of "what is." One cannot observe what is actually going on if you say my belief dictates the observation, my conditioning dictates the observation. Then it is avoidance of the understanding of "what is."

I wonder if you've got it. Are we doing this? Actually doing it—seeing, perceiving what is actual, your actual belief, your actual sense of dependency, your actual competitiveness, and not moving away from but observing it? That observation is not personal. But if you say "I must," or "I must not," or "I must be better than that," then it becomes personal and therefore relative. Whereas if we can look at what is actually taking place, there is then complete avoidance of any form of illusion.

Can we do this? You may agree verbally, but can we actually perceive our dependency, whether on a person, a belief, an ideal, or on some experience that has given us a great deal of excitement? That dependence will inevitably create illusion. So can we observe the fact that we are dependent?

So in the same way we are going to find out if there is such a thing as absolute truth—if you are interested in this, because this has been asked not only by the present questioner, but by monks who have given their life to this, by philosophers, by every religious person who is not institutionalized, but is deeply concerned with life, with reality and truth. So if one is really concerned about what truth is, one has to go into it very, very deeply.

First of all, one has to understand what reality is. What is reality? That which you perceive, that which you touch, that which you taste, when you have pain, and so on. So reality is sensation and the reaction to that sensation, the response to the sensation as an idea, and that idea is created by thought. So thought has created reality—the marvelous architecture, the great cathedrals of the world, the temples, the mosques, and the idols that are put in them, the images, all are created by thought. And we say, that is reality, because you can touch it, you can taste it, you can smell it.

Q: What about hallucinations? This can be a disturbance in the physiological brain.

K: Of course, sir. Hallucinations, illusions, delusions take place when the brain is damaged, when there is an avoidance of or an escape from "what is." All these words, illusions, hallucination, delusions, are all of that category.

So we are saying that all the things that thought has created— the knowledge, the acquisition of knowledge through science, through mathematics, and so on—are reality. But nature is not created by thought. That tree, the mountains, the rivers, the wa- ters, the deer, the snake, is not created by thought; it is there. But out of the tree we make a chair; that's created by thought. So thought has created the actual world in which we live, but nature, including the environment, is obviously not created by thought.

Then we ask, is truth reality? One perceives that thought has created the world in which we live, but thought has not created the universe. Thought can inquire into the universe. The cosmol- ogists, the astrophysicists, pursue their inquiry through thought, and they will come to certain conclusions, certain hypotheses, and try to prove those hypotheses, always through thought. So thought is relative, and therefore, whatever it creates, in whatever direction it moves, it must be relative, it must be limited.

Please, this is not a lecture, I am not a professor—thank God! We are just inquiring as two human beings wanting to find out what truth is, if there is such a thing.

So the mind is no longer in illusion, that is the first thing. It has no hypotheses, no hallucinations, no delusions, it doesn't want to grasp something, or create an experience that it calls truth— which most people do. So the mind has now brought order into itself. It has order, there is no confusion due to illusions, delusions, hallucinations, experiences. So the mind, the brain, has lost its capacity to create illusions. Right? Then what is truth? That is, what is the relationship between reality—in the sense that we have explained—and that which is not created by thought? Is there something that is not the product of thought? Can we go on with this?

That is, are our minds now, sitting here under these trees, on a rather cool day, are our minds free from every form of illusion? Otherwise you cannot possibly find out the other. Which means—is your mind completely free of any confusion? So that it is absolute order. Because how can a confused, disorderly mind, a mind that is in turmoil, ever find what truth is? It can invent. It can say, there is truth, or there is no truth. But only a mind that has a sense of absolute order, a mind that is completely free from every form of illusion, can proceed to find out.

There is something rather interesting here, if you are interested in it. The astrophysicists, the scientists, are using thought to find out, going outward. They are investigating the world around them, matter, always moving outward. But if you start inward, the "me" is also matter—thought is matter—so if you can go inward, then you are moving from fact to fact. Therefore, you begin to discover that which is beyond matter. That's up to you.

This is a very serious affair; it is not just something for an hour one morning. One has to give one's life to this, not move away from life. Life is my struggles, anxiety, fears, boredom, loneliness, sorrow—you follow?—my misfortunes, all the regrets—all that is my life. I must understand that and go through that, not move away from it. Then, if you have gone through it, there is such a thing as absolute truth.

There Is Only Infinite Watching

———

MARY ZIMBALIST: Sir, are you saying that inquiry must continue, that you don't arrive at a point where you stop inquiring, or where you have an answer, so-called, but there is a continuing spirit of inquiry?

KRISHNAMURTI: This is a rather difficult question to answer. Do you inquire further if you come to something that has no space, no time? You see, when we talk about inquiry, who is the inquirer? We come back to that old thing. The inquirer is the inquired into. I don't know if I am making myself clear on this point. When I inquire into matter, through a telescope, through all kinds of experiments, I am inquiring. But the person who inquires is different there from the thing he is inquiring into. That is clear. But here, in the subjective world, in the world of the psyche, the inquirer is part of the psyche; he is not separate from the psyche. If that is clear, then the inquirer has quite a different meaning.

MZ: Are you saying that then there is only inquiry, there is no inquired, or inquirer?

K: No, I would say there is only infinite watching. There is no watcher in watching, but extraordinary vitality and energy in watching, because you have watched the whole psychological, subjective world. And now when you are watching, there is no background which is watching; there is only watching "as is." You see, that means with great attention, and in that attention there is no entity who is attending; there is only attention that has space, that is totally quiet, silent, that has a tremendous gathering of energy, and therefore, there is a total absence of self-interest. Now is that possible for a human being?

Human beings find this terribly difficult, so you come along and say, "Look, my friend, do this, and this, and this, and you'll get that. I'll be your guru." Then I call you my spiritual authority, and I am lost, I am caught again. This has been the process, you can see it wherever there are the saints, a spiritual hierarchy that recognizes the saint, and this process goes on all the time. So man has been incapable of standing on his own feet. He wants to rely on something, whether it is his wife, a job, a belief, or some extraordinary experience he may have had.

So I am saying that there must be complete freedom. That freedom is not so complicated. There is that freedom when there is no self-interest at all. Because self-interest is very small, very petty, very narrow, and unless there is complete freedom from that, truth becomes impossible. And truth cannot be through any path; it is a pathless land. You can't go through any system, any method, any form of meditation to reach it. There is really no reaching it—it is.

A Man Addicted to Knowledge Cannot Find the Truth

———

LET US REALLY GO into this question of there being various paths leading to ultimate reality. A path can lead only to that which is known, and that which is known is not the truth. When you know something, it ceases to be truth because it is past, it is entirely arrested. Therefore, the known, the past, is caught in the net of time. Accordingly it is not the truth, it is not the real. So a path leading to the known cannot lead you to truth, and a path can lead only to the known and not to the unknown. You take a path to a house in a village, because you know where that house is, and there are many paths to your house and to your village. But reality is the immeasurable, the unknown. If you could measure it, it would not be truth. And what you have learned through books, through the say-so of others, is not real; it is only repetition, and what is repeated is no longer truth.

So is there any path to truth? We have thought so far that all paths lead to truth. Do they? Does the path of the ignorant, the path of the man with ill will lead to truth? He must abandon all paths, mustn't he? Can a man who is concerned with murdering people in the name of the state find truth unless he abandons his occupation? So all paths do not lead to truth. A man who is addicted to the acquiring of knowledge cannot find truth because he is concerned with knowledge and not with truth. The man who accepts division, will he find truth? Obviously not, because he has chosen a particular path and not the whole. Will the man of action find reality? Obviously not, for the simple reason that by following a part, we cannot find the whole.

This means that knowledge, division, and action separately cannot lead anywhere but to destruction, to illusion, to restlessness. This is what has happened. The man who has pursued knowledge for the sake of knowledge, believing that it would lead him to reality, becomes a scientist, yet what has science done to the world? I am not decrying science. The scientist is like you and me; he differs from us only in his laboratory. Otherwise he is like you and me with his narrowness, his fears, his nationalism.

To believe that there is a path that "masters" teach "disciples" is also rather fantastic, isn't it? Because wisdom is not found through a disciple or through a master. Happiness is not found except by abandoning the idea that we are the chosen few who travel along a special path. This idea merely gives us a sense of security, of aggrandizement. The idea that yours is the direct path and that ours will take more time is the outcome of immature thinking. Does it not divide mankind into systematized paths?

Those that are mature will find the truth. He who is mature never pursues either the path of "masters" or the path of knowledge, of science, of devotion, or of action. A man who is committed to any particular path is immature, and such a man will never find the eternal, the timeless, because the particular path to which he is committed belongs to time. Through time you can never find the timeless. Through misery you can never find happiness. Misery must be set aside if happiness is to be. If you love, in that love there can be no contention and no conflict. In the midst of darkness there is no light, and when you get rid of darkness, you have light. Similarly, love is when there is no possessiveness, when there is no condemnation, when there is no self-fulfillment.

Those of us who are committed to paths have vested mental, emotional, and physical interests, and that is why we find it extremely difficult to become mature. How can we abandon that to which we have clung for the past fifty or sixty years? How can you leave your house and become once more a beggar, just as you were when you were really seeking? Now you have committed yourself to an organization of which you are the head, the secretary, or a member. To the man who is seeking, the search itself is love, that itself is devotion, that itself is knowledge. The man who has committed himself to a particular path or action is caught up in systems, and he will not find truth. Through the part the whole is never found. Through a little crack of the window we do not see the sky, the marvelous clear sky, and the man who can see the sky clearly is the man who is in the open, away from all paths, from all traditions.

There Is No Technique

KRISHNAMURTI: We are having a dialogue, which means a conversation between people who are concerned about certain problems of human beings and want to go into them deeply, with care and affection, not with any form of assertion or argument. A dialectical method seeks to find out the truth through opinions. But we are not investigating dialectically. Rather, we are like two friends talking over their human problems together who hope to solve them and discover truth.

You see, I am afraid there is a great deal of misapprehension that we are trying to find a technique to truth, which means learning, practicing a method that will help you to come upon truth. We deny that there is any such technique. Please be very clear on this. Technique implies learning a method. Of course, to send a spacecraft to Mars, which is a most extraordinary feat, you need a great deal of technology, of accumulated knowledge, of "know-how." But as truth is a pathless land, it is a pathless land, you can't lay down a line, a direction, a path to it, and then practice it, discipline yourself, learn a technique.

So we are not offering or talking about a technique, a method, or a system. We are already so mechanically minded that we think that by practicing a technique, verbal repetition, silence, that this will somehow loosen or free the mind from all mechanistic activity. I am afraid it won't. What we are saying is that you must have the interest, the drive, the intensity to find out—to find out for yourself—not be told how to do it. Then what you discover is yours; then you will be free from all gurus, all techniques, all authority. Please bear that in mind while we are having a dialogue about these matters.

(The audience then put a series of questions that Krishnamurti summarized.)

KRISHNAMURTI: You would like to have a dialogue about understanding, about the relationship between speech, word, thought, and silence, and the responsibility one has not to form an image in relationship. Those were the questions that were put. Also, about vulnerability and whether we can we live without a motive. Now which of those questions shall we take so that we can think or observe or trace it right to the end, not be diverted in other directions, go to the very end of one question which may include all other questions?

QUESTIONER: Understanding.

K: Understanding, right. I think that is good; I would take that too myself. What do we mean by that word *understanding*? Please go into it slowly, not quickly. What does the understanding of something imply? Is it verbal understanding, comprehension through verbal description, comprehension through affection—I like you, I am your friend, I tell you something, therefore you understand what I am saying? Or is it an insight into something that is rather complex and confused? Or how does understanding take place? Does understanding take place through verbal communication, which is description? If you and I are speaking English or French or Italian or whatever, is it through that verbal communication and description that there is an understanding or an insight? Or does understanding take place not merely through words, not merely through description, but through going beyond the word, which means both you and the other are free of the verbal structure which is the nature of thought, and are penetrating that and having an insight?

When we talk about a car, that is very simple. I have observed it; I have played with it and know how it works. I understand, I know, how to climb that mountain. But we are talking of under-standing psychologically, not mere worldly understanding, but much more deeply, the understanding which brings about an insight. An insight means having sight into something, which then becomes the truth. And I can never go back from it. When I understand something, I have an insight into it, and therefore, that very insight will wipe away any misunderstanding, any complexity; I have clarity about it.

So understanding implies, doesn't it, that the mind, the brain, the whole structure of the mind, listens not only to the words but goes beyond them and sees the deep meaning of that particular statement. Then there is an insight, and then you say, "I understand it. I have got it." So insight implies a mind that is quiet, willing to listen, to go beyond the word, and to observe the truth of something.

Say, for instance, the speaker makes a statement like, "The ending of sorrow is the beginning of wisdom." He makes that statement. Now how do you receive it? Please listen. How do you receive it? What is your reaction to it? Do you make an abstraction out of it and with that abstraction, which is an idea, try to understand what he said? Or do you listen—that is, do you listen to the word, the meaning of the word, and go beyond the word and see the truth or the falseness of that statement? Not how to end sorrow, or how to have wisdom, but whether that statement conveys a truth or a falsehood. To observe the truth or the falsehood, your mind must be quiet, and then you have an insight into it; then you say, "By Jove, how true that is." So in the same way, understanding implies having an insight into a problem. Right? So that you go beyond all arguments, all dialectical approaches—it is so, it is immovable.

Say, for instance, the speaker says, "There is no technique to truth; truth is a pathless land." He makes that statement, he made it fifty years ago, and how do you receive that? Go on. How do you receive that statement? This is a dialogue. Do you receive it with an opinion, saying, "That can't be true because everybody talks about technique, methods, a system," and now this man comes along and says, "There is no path, there is no technique to truth." So you say, "Well, who is right—is this man right, or is the other one?" So are you arguing, comparing, judging, or do you listen to that statement, not knowing what is right and wrong? Because, actually, you don't know, do you? Ten people, or a million people, have said, "There is a technique," and someone comes along and says, "There is no technique whatsoever." This man may be totally wrong!

But he explains what he means. A technique implies practice, time, a mechanistic process. Our minds are already mechanistic enough, and this is making them more mechanistic. So he explains all that, and you still say, "A thousand people have techniques." Do you balance these two and then say, "Well, I prefer that rather than this"? Or do you receive what he said in complete, objective silence, quietly, not knowing what is truth? And when you do listen quietly, which means with complete attention, then you discover, have an insight into what is being said, and then it is yours, not mine. I don't know if you see this—that is, to find out what is true and what is false, to find out the truth in the false. So your mind must be extraordinarily open, vulnerable. I wonder if we are understanding each other.

You Have to Find Truth through the Mirror of Relationship

———

KRISHNAMURTI: Suppose that yesterday my wife said something to me, nagged, bullied, or was happy with me, gave me some comfort, etc., and thought has built an image about her. And I live according to that image; and she does too, according to her image of me. So I say to myself, why does thought do this? Don't answer it yet, please, give two minutes to go into it. You can only do that it if you have no ideas about it, if you don't say, this is so, that is so, and rush immediately into words. So we have to find out why thought does this. Thought does it because it finds security in the image. I am secure in the image of my wife. Wait a minute, just listen to it. My country—right?—security, my group. Security. The image that I have created about the group, or about the nation, or the image that I have created through religious indoctrination—whether of Christ or the Hindu gods. And so thought creates these images because it finds security in them. Whether that security is found in neuroticism, neurotic beliefs, or some beautiful fanciful image, it is the same process. So thought finds security, wants security. Why?

QUESTIONER: It seems to me thought wants to maintain itself, that thought is impermanent and therefore seeks safety.

K: Yes, go on, sir, a little further, don't stop there. You have said something, investigate, move with it. Are you sure of what you are saying? Don't theorize about it. Unless you are speaking from fact, everything else is meaningless.

Q: Safety, security, and certainty.

K: Which means what? To be certain, safe, all that means it demands complete, inviolable security. Just a minute. Why? Why does thought demand this? In the case of my wife, for example, I possess her, she is mine, etc. In that there is great certainty, great security. I have identified myself with her. She has fulfilled what I want. And she does the same with me; it's a mutual, interacting exploitation. Sorry to use such an ugly word, but it is a fact. So I say to myself, thought seeks security, but is there security in the image? I sought security in my wife, or girl, and I have built an image about her, and in that image there is security for me. But it's an image. You understand? It's a word, a memory, such a fragile thing, but yet I hold on to it.

Q: Sir, I am aware of the passage of time, and I'm afraid it's going to end, so I seek permanency in the images I create.

K: Permanency is sought in anything. So I am asking, why does thought seek it? Look into it. I seek security in the traditional symbol, in the cross, I seek security in that. The cross, the whole structure, and all that lies behind it, rituals, dogma, all that, I find security in that—why? And I know logically, if I am aware at all, logically, that it is a product of thought. And yet thought clings to it—why?

Q: Conditioning.

K: Is that part of our conditioning? Part of our being conditioned from childhood to believe in the symbol—Rama, Krishna, or Christ. Why? Thought finds security in it, yet when thought looks into it, I say, my God, there is no security there; it is just an idea—which thought has put together. So when thought clings to an image, it is the very essence of neuroticism. I know it is danger, and yet I cling to it. Do you see the absurdity of this?

Q: Yes, I do.

K: No, wait a minute, do you actually see the absurdity of it?

Q: Yes, I do.

K: Then it's the end of it. Then you don't create images. But wait. If my wife calls me an idiot, will I listen to her without forming an image? Or will it be the old tradition, habit, conditioning, the response of image-making? You follow? She calls me an idiot, but there is no image-making. Is that possible? Or when she flatters me, which is the same thing, the other side of the coin. Shall we go into this? That is, my wife calls me an idiot because I said or did something which she didn't like. Thought is conditioned, so the immediate response is an image. I am not an idiot. There is an image. Now can I listen to her—please find out—can I listen to her without that response? Which does not mean with indifference. Can I listen to her when she says "Darling, you are marvelous"—which is another image? Can I listen to her, both when she calls me an idiot and when she calls me marvelous, without storing, without registering it? Do you understand my question? It is very important; do get this a little bit. The mechanism of the brain is to register. Right? It is registering. And it is so conditioned that it registers "idiot" immediately. Or when she says what a marvelous person I am, "marvelous" is registered. Now can there be no registering, when she calls me an idiot or she calls me marvelous? Which doesn't mean I become indifferent, hard, and callous. Now I can only do that—please listen—I can only not register, that is only possible, when I give my complete attention to what she says. Whether she calls me an idiot or marvelous, when I pay complete attention, there is no registering.

Do it, please, as you are sitting there, do it now. That is, you have got an image about your wife or your girlfriend, or your boyfriend—gosh, this boy and girl, man and woman, I'm getting bored with this! We go on about it until we die, it's so silly. I am pointing out that image-making is the process of thought. Thought has made the image, so there is conflict in that. And I see the tremendous danger in conflict, whether between India and Pakistan or Russia and America. There is tremendous danger because people kill each other. So I ask, can that image-making stop? It can. Why does thought bring about these images? It finds security, safety, in these images—and yet thought knows how absurd that is. And when thought clings to something that is irrational, it is neurotic.

Human Beings Have Built in Themselves Images as a Fence of Security

————

WE ARE INQUIRING TOGETHER into the question of relationship. Man cannot exist without relationship. Life is relationship and action. These two are fundamental to man. What is our present relationship with another? What is your relationship with your wife? Or your relationship with your husband? What is your relationship with your Buddhist or Hindu or Christian priest? What is your relationship?

When you examine it closely, your relationship is based on images—the image that you have built about God, about Buddha, about your wife, and the image your wife has built about you. That is a fact, isn't it? Images in marriage, which is the most intimate relationship, occur daily; the man creates an image about his wife and the wife creates an image about him, and the relationship is between these two images. Would you agree to that?

These images are built through daily contact, sex, irritation, comfort, and so on. Each one builds his own image about another and also has an image about himself. He has an image too about God, about his religious deity, because when you create an image, there is security in that image, however false, however unreal, however insane. In the image that the mind has created, there is security. When you create an image about your wife, or your wife about you, the image is not the actual. But it is much more difficult to live with the actual, much easier to live with the image.

So relationship is between images, and therefore, there is no relationship at all. I hope you are following all this. This is a fact. The Christian worships an image. That image is created through the centuries by the priest, by the worshiper who says: I need comfort, security, somebody to look after me; I am in a mess, confused, insecure, and in that image I find security. We have become image worshipers, not worshipers of truth, not worshipers of righteous life, but worshipers of images, the national image with its flag, the image that you have of the scientist, of the government, and so on. Image-making is one of the human failings. Now is it possible to have no image about anything, but to live only with facts, the fact being that which is actually happening? Are we meeting each other?

Why does the mind create an image? Life isn't an image. Life is strife, unfortunately. Life is constant conflict. Conflict is not an image. It is a fact, that which is happening. So why does the mind create images? The speaker means by an image, a symbol, a concept, a conclusion, an ideal. These are all images—that is, what I should be; I am not this, but I would like to be that. That is an image projected by the mind in time, projected into the future. So that is unreal. What is real is what is actually taking place now in your mind. Can we go on from there?

We are asking, why does the mind create an image? Is it because in the image there is security? If I have a wife, I create an image about her. The very word *wife* is an image. But my wife is a living thing, a changing, vital, human entity. To understand her requires much more attention, greater energy, but I think if I have an image about her, it is much easier to live with that image.

First of all, don't you have an image about yourself? That you are a great man or not a great man, that you are this, that, and so on? When you live with images, you are living with illusions, not with reality. Now, what is the mechanism of making images? All organized, accepted, respectable religions have always had some kind of image. And mankind, with the help of the priest, has always worshiped the symbol, the idea, the concept, and so on.

In that worship he finds comfort, safety, security. But the image is the projection of thought. And to understand the nature and making of images, you must understand the whole process of thinking. May we go into that? Will you come with me? Good!

So what is thinking? That is what you are doing all day long. Your cities are built on thinking; your armaments are based on thinking. The politicians are based on thinking, your religious leaders, everything in the world is based on thinking. The poets may write beautiful verse, but the thinking process goes on. So one must inquire, if you are serious, and are willing to go into the question, what is thinking? You are thinking now.

We were saying that man has habitually made images, especially in the religious world, and he has also images about himself, and we are asking why does the mind, your mind, make images? Is it because in images there is security, however false the images are, without any reality? Man apparently seeks security in an illusion. So to understand image-making, which is common to all mankind, one has to go into the nature of thinking and thought. All thought. Thought has not created nature. The tiger, the river, the marvelous trees, the forest and the mountains, the shadows, valleys, and the beauty of the Earth, man has not created that. But man has created through thought the destructive machinery of war, and also great medical, surgical progress, and instant communication, and so on. Thought has been responsible for a great deal of good and a great deal of harm. That is a fact. And a man who is serious wants to inquire whether thought is ever capable of reducing any of the problems we have. So are you serious enough to find out for yourself what thinking is?

Thinking is the response of memory, stored up in the brain as knowledge. Knowledge comes from experience. Mankind has had thousands of experiences from which it has accumulated a great deal of knowledge, some of it factual and some of it illusory or neurotic. And when you are asked a question, that memory responds as thought. This is a fact. We have discussed this matter with many scientists; some of them agree, others don't. But you can find this out for yourself: that is, you have an experience, that experience is stored in the memory as knowledge, and that remembered knowledge projects thought. Is this clear? Don't agree with me, please. Examine it for yourself. Look into yourself. If you have no experience, no knowledge, no memory, you can't think. So there is knowledge through experience, stored in the memory, and the response of that memory, which is thought, to a challenge—and on that thought we live.

But knowledge is always limited. There is no complete knowledge about anything. This is a fact. So thought is always limited, however beautiful it is—for thought may build a cathedral, a marvelous statue, a great poem, a great epic, and so on. But thought born of knowledge must always be limited because knowledge is always incomplete, knowledge is always in the shadow of ignorance. So thought has created these images, thought has created the image between you and your wife, thought has created the idea of nationality with its technology which is destroying the world, and so on.

Now we are asking the question: is it possible to live one's daily life without a single image? Thought must function to go from here to your home. You must have knowledge of where your home is, the road you take, and so on. That knowledge must exist, otherwise you would get completely lost. Knowledge is necessary to speak a language, for the speaker to speak English, and so on. But is it necessary to create an image at all? You understand my question? Can we live without a single image? Which means without any belief—which doesn't mean you lead a chaotic life—but without any belief, without any ideal, without any concept, all of these being projections of thought and therefore all limited? This raises the question: what is action? Because action based on thought is always incomplete. Therefore, one has to ask: is there an action which under all circumstances is correct? Because this is a very serious matter.

The Burden of These Images Dominates Thinking, Relationships, and Daily Life

KRISHNAMURTI: I see first of all that the mind is lazy and likes to live in a rut—the rut being belief, opinion, conclusion. Say that I've talked to several people, and they've formed an opinion about somebody, and you can't shake them—you show them the facts, the logic, the truth of those, but nothing doing, because their opinion is right. Haven't you met such people all your life? Christ exists and that's the end of it; Marx is right and that's the end of it; the Little Red Book is marvelous and that's the end of it. Now why does the mind do this? Because it finds in the Red Book, in Marx, in Jesus, complete security, which means complete laziness—it doesn't have to think anymore. And it's afraid to learn any more, because to learn something more means disturbing "what is," your conclusion, your image. So I see that the brain likes to live in security, in abstractions, which are then more important than the fact. I have formed an opinion about you, rightly or wrongly, and that opinion is a conclusion, and to change that and say, "By Jove, I'm mistaken; you are different" needs a little thought, a little energy—that is, I don't want to be wrong, I would rather you be wrong.

So the brain says, "I want security, and my security is in a belief, a conclusion, and don't disturb it." Right? So having found a belief and imagining it has found security and therefore becoming lazy, it doesn't want to be disturbed. Watch your own mind, not mine—I haven't been through all this mess.

QUESTIONER: It seems to me that when one observes something—say, a mountain in all its glory—one receives an impression. Can you tell us what such an impression is? It doesn't necessarily leave an image.

K: Of course, an impression. I have an impression about the mountains, I have an impression about you—I don't know you, I have an impression, a vague feeling, you have impressed me, you have left a pleasant or unpleasant mark on me. Next time I meet you, that impression is strengthened, and I say, "By Jove, he's a nice chap" or not a nice chap, and then from that, a third time, the image is established. Please look at it—the brain would rather live in an abstraction, in which it finds security, and even if it is very disturbing, that is the only security it has.

So the brain needs security. And therefore, the image becomes the most important thing. I have formed a conclusion that there is no life after death, or there is life after death, which gives me tremendous comfort, so don't talk anymore about it. I live in that belief. It gives me tremendous security—whether that belief is neurotic, real, or illusory doesn't matter. So I've found out that an image about you, about anything, gives security to the mind, to the brain, which therefore clings to it. And that's what is the matter with all of you.

Q: Must we not find out if there is such a thing as security, or is it just another concept?

K: I'm coming to that. As I said, the brain needs security, otherwise you can't function properly. Like a child given complete security, it's happy, it learns quicker. And when the family is broken up, when the father and mother are quarreling, the poor child feels lost, neurotic, and becomes violent, begins to shoot, kill people. You've seen all this. So do you find security in an image? Go into it, be aware of it, don't talk about a good image or a bad image—do you have images, conclusions, in which you take security—do you?

Q: Temporary security. Or if you are separated from a loved one, you have an image.

K: Yes—temporary security when you are separated from your beloved—when you love somebody in America and you're here and you feel separated, and therefore, you have an image about him and temporarily that image gives you comfort. But my beloved in America might be chasing another girl!

Q: Sir, the whole of science is based on images, and that's natural.

K: Let's keep it simple, it's complex enough. Do you have an image in which the brain, your mind, your feelings have established a vested interest, and so it is clung to, and you won't drop it? And therefore, your mind is lazy. Then you say to yourself, "How am I to stop image-making? How am I not to conclude at any time, but always to have a mind that is completely free, so that it meets everything anew—the tree, you, everything anew, fresh, free?" I have seen how the machinery of thought builds the image. Have you seen it? Have you really seen it? Have you observed, have you had an insight into image-making? If you have an insight into it, you won't make any image at all, because the insight is security. Do you get it?

Q: Is it your memory that makes you aware of the image?

K: No, from the first time I meet you, I've an impression, pleasant or unpleasant, about you. That impression may be very slight, like a faint footprint on the sands, but the next time I meet you, that footprint has taken a little more shape. And the third time it's solid. Now that impression has become stronger through my contact with you, but if I had had no impression, I would have to look at you each time anew, to watch you, listen to you, to feel you anew each time—which is much more troublesome, rather than simply saying, "I've an image about you, you are this—finished." And having established that image, it gives me security and I don't want to learn anything more about you.

Have you understood this so far? Understood—that means do you have insight into this, therefore you have dropped your laziness and your image. Have you? If you have not, why not, what's wrong? You've spent money, energy to get here, sitting in this hot tent, and you leave it today with your images intact. What's the point of it? Why do you go on when you see for yourself the stupidity, the lack of security in the things in which you have put your faith? Look, if you have stocks, when you see danger in the stock market, don't you sell? Don't you buy something which is much more secure? Why don't you do the same here—not that this is a stock market!

Q: Sir, if I drop my beliefs, my images, now that I've seen them, there is nothing left. And I'm scared of having nothing.

K: I see if I drop my images, my conclusions, my laziness, I've nothing left and I'm frightened. Why do you drop them? Because somebody else says drop them? Or do you drop them because you have insight, because you have an understanding of this, and therefore, your understanding is your security? Then there is no fear. Once you have the key of observation, which is insight, which is the capacity to look, to understand intelligently, then that intelligence is security. And because you're lazy, you don't have it.

So observation means nonabstraction. There is only observation, not the observer, who is an abstraction. The observer is an abstraction, an idea, a conclusion, is the past. And through the eyes of the past you are looking at the trees, the mountains, your wife, your children, and all the rest of it. And that is part of your laziness. Now to see that, to have an insight into it, to be aware of this extraordinary structure of illusion, which is an abstraction, that observation in itself is total security. Have you got it?

So can you leave this tent this morning happily, free of all the images, and therefore only have this light of insight? Do you?

A questioner has pointed out that the mountains and the trees, the rivers and the green meadows are different from man, and the mass of people. So what is my relationship with the mass? What is my relationship with this total, seething mankind, with all its miseries, and all the rest of it? Is it laziness that prevents me finding out my relationship with it? Is it my indifference? Or in asking that very question, have I activated my energy to find out? Don't look at me, what do you say? The lady says it's easy to talk about the hills, the trees and mountains and flowers, but when it comes to human relationship, whether with one or many, life becomes very difficult. It is difficult, as we said, because we have no relationship with anything—we have relationship in abstraction. And therefore, we live in abstractions—the mass, the "me," the conclusion, the image—we live in abstractions. Do you realize what that means? We don't live at all—but in images, in conclusions that have no value!

Q: Sir, how can we get rid of all that?

K: I've shown it to you. Look, let us keep it very simple. When you see a physical danger, you react, don't you? Why? When you see danger, you react instantly, because you are conditioned to the danger, whether it's a wild animal, a bus, or somebody trying to hit you, you react instantly. That is, you react instantly according to your conditioning. And you are conditioned now psychologically, mentally, intellectually in the brain cells, you are conditioned to live in speculations, in concepts, in formulas—you're conditioned to that, and you don't see the danger of it. If you saw the danger of it as you see the danger of a wild animal, you'd drop it instantly. So you say, "I don't see the danger of it; therefore, I can't drop it. How will you help me to see the danger of it?" Are you doing the work, or am I? I am doing the work; you are just listening. You're not working.

You say, "Now tell me how to break down these images." That is, you are not exercising your energy to find out. That means you are being lazy, and want to be told. Then you can say, "Well, I agree or disagree, it's not practical." So you play with it. But if you say, "Look, I want to find out," because you see the truth of it—that you can't live with images because they are destructive, dangerous—that is another matter. And to see that, you must have energy, you must work; it isn't something to be told by another. I've told you, but you don't put your vitality into it.

So a mind, a brain, which is old, conditioned, and always living in the past or projecting the future from the past, cannot face something that is living, because it means you have to apply, to move, to watch. And so the mind says, "Please, I am lazy, don't, I'd rather live with my images, I like to be comfortable." That's all you want. But to find the truth, you have to live tremendously, with no security other than the security in intelligence that comes through insight. Then you can also be a first-class technician, because you don't project your image into doing your technical job. And then you have a marvelous relationship with each other.

Freedom from Being
a Slave to the Past

―――

IRST OF ALL, WHAT is the meaning of these talks? Either
you treat the speaker as your authority from whom you are
going to learn, which is not his intention at all, at any time, at any
level; or we come together to talk things over amicably, exposing
ourselves inwardly, because this offers an opportunity to uncover
and discover and go beyond. That is the intention of these talks,
not that the speaker is laying down a law, a dogma, an authority,
a belief, a way. But rather in speaking together, we are listening
to ourselves rather than to someone else. And in listening to ourselves, we discover an infinite lot, a great depth to all our words
and meanings. At least, that is the intention.

If we treat these discussions merely as an intellectual, verbal
battle of opinions, then I am afraid they will be of very little
value. What we are concerned with, seeing the misery, the confusion within ourselves and the world, the incessant battle between
man and man, is whether there is a different way of living altogether, not merely in certain economic or social areas. Can one
live a totally different life in all the areas? That is why we come
together. To learn is to listen, not only to the speaker, but to the
nearby river. Listen to it as we are talking, listen to the boy who
is shouting, listen to your own thoughts, to your own feelings, so

that you become completely familiar with them. Becoming familiar is to understand; and to understand there must be caring to
listen, not only to your opinions, because you know very well
what your opinions are. Your opinions are your prejudices, your
pleasures, the conditions under which you have been brought up.
One must also listen to all the impacts, if one can, of the outward
influences and one's reaction to them; and through this listening,
seeing, there comes a learning. That is also the intention of these
discussions.

The question was asked whether it is possible to meditate
throughout the day without making meditation into some squalid
affair of ten minutes or an hour or two, but to sustain it throughout the day, and through this meditation to understand the nature
of dying, and what it means to live anew.

The question was also asked whether it is possible to put an
end to all the unconscious or conscious traumas, drives, compulsions. For the time being, let us limit ourselves to those questions.
And in discussing, talking over, meditation, perhaps we shall include the way of dying to everything so that the mind is made
new, and understand also the compulsive urges that we human
beings have.

That word *meditation* must be used very guardedly, with a great
deal of hesitation, because in the Western world—and dividing
the world into the West and the East is a great pity—*meditation*
has very little meaning. The West is more familiar with the word
contemplation. I think contemplation and meditation are two different things. In the East, meditation is something that one practices
day after day, according to a certain method and pattern laid
down by some authority, ancient or modern; and in following
that pattern, one learns to conquer, control thought, and go beyond. That is the meaning generally implied by that word. The
West is not so familiar with that meaning.

So let us put aside for the moment both the East and the West,
and try to find out not how to meditate but the quality of a mind
that is awake, aware, intense, that has no trauma, no suppression
nor indulgence, that is not controlling itself all the time or at
any time, that is free and therefore never lives in the shadow of
yesterday. That is what we are going to consider. We must begin

to understand this right from the beginning, because the first step matters much more than the last step. Freedom is not at the end, but at the beginning, and that is one of the most difficult things to understand. Without freedom there is no movement except within a very, very restricted area, that restriction being based on the image or the idea of organized pleasure.

I am not laying down the law or telling you what to do or not to do, or that you must agree or disagree, but we have to see the idea, the principle, the image from which all thinking begins, from which all our reactions come. Without understanding that, it is not possible to be free to go far beyond the present limitations of the mind or the limitations of the society or culture in which we have been brought up. So, if I may suggest, in listening, you each have a double task, not only to listen to the speaker but also to listen to yourself.

We all want wider and deeper experiences, experiences that are more intense, more alive, not repetitive; and so we seek them through drugs, through meditation or through visions, through becoming much more sensitive. The drugs help one, for the time being, to become extraordinarily sensitive. The whole organism is heightened. The nerves and the whole being are liberated from the pettiness of daily existence, and that brings about a great intensity. In that state of intensity, it can happen that there is no experiencer or experience, there is only the thing. In watching a flower, there is only the flower: there is no watcher watching the flower. These various forms of drugs give the body, the whole organism, and hence the brain, an extraordinary sensitivity. In that state, if you are a poet, if you are an artist, if you are this or that, you have an experience according to your temperament.

Please, I have not taken any drug, because to me any form of stimulant—any form, including your being stimulated by the speaker—be it drink, or sex, or drugs, or going to Mass and getting into a certain state of emotional tension, is utterly detrimental, because any form of stimulant, however subtle, makes the mind dull through its dependence on that stimulant. The stimulant establishes a certain habit and makes the mind dull.

Most of us do not use drugs, but we do want wider and deeper experiences. So we meditate. We hope by meditation, by control of thought, by learning, by getting into some peculiar emotional, psychological, mystical state, by having visions, experiences, to reach an extraordinary state. If you are using meditation as a means to something, then meditation becomes another drug. It creates a habit, and therefore destroys the subtlety, the sensitivity, the quality of the free mind.

Most of us like systems to follow, and there are so many systems in Asia which have been transported, I don't know why, to the West. Everyone gets trapped in those systems. There are mantras and all the rest of it. The constant repetition of words, in Latin, Sanskrit, or any other language, makes the mind quiet, but dull and stupid. A petty little mind repeating a Christian prayer is still a petty little mind. It can repeat ten million times a day; it is still a narrow, shallow, stupid mind.

Meditation is something entirely different. In order to understand it, we must put away drugs and reject all methods, including the repetition of words in order to reach some peculiar state of silence, which is really stagnation. We must also put away every form of desire for further experience. This is very difficult, because most of us are so saturated with the ugliness, brutality, violence, and despair of life that we want something more. We are longing for new experiences, whether outward experiences such as going to Mass, or inward deeper experiences. But one has to put all of these away. Only then is there freedom. The manner of putting away these things is of great importance. I can put away wanting this or that, because it is too silly; but inwardly I may still want experiences.

I may not want to see Christ or Buddha, or this or that person, that's too obviously silly, because it's a projection of one's own background. I may rationally, logically reject that. But inwardly I want my own experience, which is not contaminated by the past. But all the experiences, all the visions that I want are contaminated by the past.

I have to understand the depth, the height, the significance, the quality of the past; and in that understanding I am dying to it, the mind is dying to it. The mind is the past; the whole structure of the brain, with all its associations, is the result of the past. It is put together by time, two million years of time; and you can't put all that away by a gesture. You have to understand it as every reaction arises. Since most of us still have a great deal of the animal in us, we have to understand all that; and to understand it, one has to be aware of it. To be aware is to watch it, listen to it, not condemn it or justify it.

By being aware outwardly and inwardly, and riding on that awareness of the outward movement as a tide that goes out and a tide that comes in, riding on that, the mind then begins to discover its own reactions, responses, demands, compulsions. To understand these demands, urges, responses, you must not condemn. If you do, then you don't understand. It's like condemning a child, because that's the easiest way to deal with the child. We condemn, and we think we understand, but we do not.

We have to find out why we condemn. Why do you condemn? Why do you rationalize? Why do you justify? Condemnation, justification, rationalization are forms of escape from the fact. The fact is there, it is what is, it is there. Why should I rationalize it? Why should I condemn it? Why should I justify it? When I do that, I am wasting energy. Therefore, to understand the fact, you must live with it completely, without any distance between the mind and the fact, because the fact is the mind.

You have rejected drugs and the urge for experience, because you understand that when you want to escape from this ugly, monstrous world into something extraordinary, such experiences become escapes from the fact. Since the mind and the brain are the result of the past, one has to understand the conscious as well as the unconscious past. One can understand it immediately, not take time, months, years, going to an analyst or analyzing oneself. One can understand the whole thing immediately, with one look, if one knows how to look. So we are going to find out how to look. One cannot look if there is any sense of condemnation, any sense of justification of what one sees. That must be completely clear. To understand a child, you can't condemn it; you must watch it, watch it while it is playing, crying, laughing, sleeping. What is more important is not the child, but how you watch the child. We are not considering now a method of looking. We are trying to understand whether it is possible, by one look—not with your vision, not with your eyes only, but an inward look—to understand the whole structure and be free of it. That is what we mean by meditation—nothing else.

The mind has come to this point because it has rejected drugs, experiences, authority, following, repetition of words, control, forcing oneself in one direction. It has looked at it, studied it, gone into it, observed it; not said it is right or wrong. What has happened? The mind has now become naturally alert and sensitive, not through drugs, not through any form of stimulant. It has become exceedingly sensitive.

Let's go into that word *sensitive*. Do you want to ask questions? Are you listening to the speaker, or are you listening to yourself as the things are being said?

QUESTIONER: As you speak, I cannot see myself.

KRISHNAMURTI: When do you see yourself? Do you ever see yourself as you are, not here, but when you go out of the tent? Do you ever see the poses, the mannerisms, the pretensions, the vanities, the wanting to impress, the what you are?

We are now trying to see what we mean by sensitivity. This is of great importance—sensitivity of the body, the organism, the brain, total sensitivity. The essence of sensitivity is to be vulnerable inwardly in the sense of not having any resistance, not having any image, any formula, not saying "This is the line I draw" and reacting from that line. That is merely a resistance. Such a mind, such an inward state of defense, resistance, acceptance, obedience, following authority, makes the mind insensitive. And fear of any kind—one of the most difficult things to be free from—makes the mind invulnerable, makes it dull and insensitive. Also, there is no sensitivity when you are seeking fame, when you are dogmatic, when you are violent, when you are in a position of authority and misuse that authority by being rude, vulgar, oppressive. All that obviously makes the mind, the whole being, insensitive. Only a mind that is vulnerable is capable of affection, love—not a mind that is jealous, possessive, dominating. So we understand now, without going into too much detail, more or less what sensitivity means. It is another thing to be in that state, not just intellectually agree or ask, "How am I to come to that state where I'm totally vulnerable, and therefore totally sensitive?" You can't come to it by some trick; you'll come to it naturally, sweetly, easily, without effort, if you understand all that we have said previously about drugs, experience, ambition, greed, envy.

There is sensitivity only when there is freedom. Freedom implies freedom per se, not freedom from something. Having understood the past, we are now considering how by one look one is free of the whole structure. To look, to observe, to be aware of the whole structure instantly, there must be sensitivity. That sensitivity is denied if there is any form of image about oneself or about what one should be, that image being based on pleasure. The mind that is seeking pleasure in any form is inviting sorrow.

The mind that is sensitive—in the sense that we are using the word, not only neurologically and biologically, but totally vulnerable inwardly, without any resistance—has an extraordinary strength, vitality, and energy, because it is not battling with life, neither accepting life nor rejecting it. When one understands this whole phenomenon, when one has gone through it all, then one look is enough to destroy the whole structure. This whole process is meditation. In understanding meditation, one has to understand control and identification. Control of thought implies resistance to every other form of thought. I want to think about one thing, but thought wanders away, like a leaf wandering aimlessly. I concentrate, I control, I make a tremendous effort to push all thought away, except that one thought. That one thought is based on an ultimate pleasure. Concentration implies exclusion, narrowness, focusing on one thing, and keeping everything else in darkness. But when one understands what it is to be attentive, with the body, the nerves, the eyes, the ears, the brain, the whole, total being . . . to be attentive to color, to thought, to one's speech— then, in that attention, there is a concentration which is not exclusion. I can attend, I can look, I can work on something without exclusion.

One must also understand identification. A child is absorbed by a toy. The toy is more fascinating than anything else, and the child is completely lost in that fascination; he becomes quiet, not mischievous, not naughty, he doesn't tear and run about. The toy has become a thing that absorbs his mind, his body, everything. The toy has absorbed him. And we also, like the child, want to be absorbed by an idea, by our images, or by the images that have been presented to us, such as Buddha or Jesus Christ. Where the mind is being absorbed, either by a drink, or by an image made by the hand or by the mind, there is no sensitivity, and therefore there is no love.

The mind that is free is really an empty mind. We only know emptiness as space with an object in it. We only know this emptiness here in the tent, because there is the outward structure of the tent, and that we call emptiness. We do not know space—not between the Earth and Mars, we are not talking about that— without an object, and therefore, we don't know what emptiness is. A mind that is not totally empty, without an object, is never free. One can understand intellectually that all desire, all relationship, all action, takes place within the space created by the object, or by the center, or by the image. In that space there is never freedom. It's like a goat tied to a post, who can wander only the length of its tether.

To understand the nature of freedom, one must understand the nature of emptiness and space, and again, all that is meditation. Only when the mind is totally empty and there is no center which creates space, and therefore there is space, is the mind completely quiet. The mind then is extraordinarily still; and it is only in stillness, which can only take place in the emptiness which is space without the object, that all energy—all energy comes into being without movement.

When energy is no longer dissipated, and comes about without any movement, there must be action. A kettle that is boiling, if it has no escape, must burst. Only when the mind is completely still, not the stillness of stagnation, but of tremendous vitality and energy, is there an event, an explosion which is creation. Writing a book, writing a poem, becoming famous, is not creation. The world is filled with books. I believe four thousand or more books are produced every week. Self-expression in no manner is creation. And a mind that is not in that state of creation is a dead mind. One must begin, if one would understand meditation, right from the beginning. And the beginning is self-knowledge. Self-knowing is the beginning of wisdom, and the ending of sorrow is the beginning of a new life.

Thought Is Always Limited

"WHY IS THOUGHT SO persistent? It seems so restless, so exasperatingly insistent. Do what you will, it is always active, like a monkey, and its very activity is exhausting. You cannot escape from it, it pursues you relentlessly. You try to suppress it, and a few seconds later it pops up again. It is never quiet, never in repose; it is always pursuing, always analyzing, always torturing itself. Sleeping or waking, thought is in constant turmoil, and it seems to have no peace, no rest."

Can thought ever be at peace? It can think about peace and attempt to be peaceful, forcing itself to be still; but can thought in itself be tranquil? Is not thought in its very nature restless? Is not thought the constant response to constant challenge? There can be no cessation to challenge, because every moment of life is a challenge; and if there is no awareness of that challenge, then there is decay, death. Challenge-and-response is the very way of life. Response can be adequate or inadequate; and it is inadequacy of response to challenge that provokes thought, with its restlessness. Challenge demands action, not verbalization. Verbalization is thought. The word; the symbol, retards action; and idea is the word, as memory is the word. There is no memory without the symbol, without the word. Memory is word, thought, and can thought be the true response to challenge? Is challenge an idea? Challenge is always new, fresh; and can thought, idea, ever be new? When thought meets the challenge, which is ever new, is not that response the outcome of the old, the past?

When the old meets the new, the meeting is inevitably incomplete; and this incompleteness is thought in its restless search for completeness. But can thought, idea, ever be complete? Thought, idea, is the response of memory; and memory is always incomplete. Experience is the response to challenge. This response is conditioned by the past, by memory; such response only strengthens the conditioning. Experience does not liberate, it strengthens belief, memory, and it is this memory that responds to challenge; so experience is the conditioner.

"But what place has thought?"

Do you mean what place has thought in action? Has idea any function in action? Idea becomes a factor in action in order to modify it, to control it, to shape it; but idea is not action. Idea, belief, is a safeguard against action; it has a place as a controller, modifying and shaping action. Idea is the pattern for action.

"Can there be action without the pattern?"

Not if one is seeking a result. Action toward a predetermined goal is not action at all, but conformity to belief, to idea. If one is seeking conformity, then thought, idea, has a place. The function of thought is to create a pattern for so-called action, and thereby to kill action. Most of us are concerned with the killing of action; and idea, belief, dogma, help to destroy it. Action implies insecurity, vulnerability to the unknown; and thought, belief, which is the known, is an effective barrier to the unknown. Thought can never penetrate into the unknown; it must cease for the unknown to be. The action of the unknown is beyond the action of thought; and thought, being aware of this, consciously or unconsciously clings to the known. The known is ever responding inadequately to the unknown, to the challenge; and from this inadequate response arise conflict, confusion, and misery. It is only when the known, the idea, ceases that there can be the action of the unknown, which is measureless.

The Content of One's Consciousness Is One's Entire Existence

———

F ROM TIME IMMEMORIAL, MAN has tried to solve the problem of living a life that is whole and that can be lived without any friction. It is true that friction brings about a certain kind of activity, but such activity does a great deal of mischief. And to live a life without friction, one must inquire very deeply into the whole problem of consciousness, which means the mind, the whole structure of our thinking, of our intellectual, moral, spiritual, organic life. So one has to go into this question: what is consciousness, in which all the activities of thought take place? The activity of thought, with all its difficulties, all its complexities, its memories, its projections into the future, is within the field of consciousness, isn't it? This consciousness which is the "me." I am using ordinary English words, not a new jargon that you have to learn.

You see, if the totality of consciousness is the result of fragmentation, that consciousness cannot possibly be aware of what it means to be whole. If my mind, which is the basis of consciousness, is fragmented, and then asked to look at the world as a whole, it has no meaning. How can a fragmented consciousness observe life as a total, nonfragmentary movement? That is why it is important to inquire into the nature of consciousness. To be conscious, to be aware, to perceive the fragmentation—and when you perceive it, is that the seeing by one fragment of other fragments? When there is such perception, it is still fragmentation. And that is what is going on all the time in our consciousness.

Now to ask such a mind to observe life, in which love, death, livelihood, relationship, the inquiry into whether there is a God or not, are all fragments—can the mind observe all that without fragmentation? So, again, it is important to ask oneself, what is consciousness? Consciousness exists only because of its content. Its content makes up consciousness. My consciousness is made up of my conditioning as a Hindu, as a Brahmin, born in India with its tradition, superstitions, beliefs, dogmas, divisions, with all the gods, and the recent acquisition of a new poison called nationalism, and so on. The conscious and unconscious residue of the past, the racial inheritance and the recent experiences, denials, and sacrifices, the temperaments, the activity of personal demands, all that is the content of my consciousness, as it is also of yours. And that content makes up our consciousness. Without it there is no consciousness.

Please, this is very important to understand, because when we go into the question of what death is and what love is, one must have understood this, otherwise it will have no meaning. When one dies, the content of the brain cells that have stored up all the memory, which make up the consciousness, withers away, with all the remembrances, experiences, knowledge. Then what has happened to consciousness as the "me" which has lived in this world, fighting, struggling, miserable, full of anxieties and endless sorrow?

The mind needs to understand the nature and structure of consciousness, that is to say, what you are, which is your consciousness. That consciousness with its content makes up the total which you call the "me," the ego, the person, the psychological structure of your temperament, your idiosyncrasies, your conditioning. One has to understand it very deeply, nonverbally, though we may use words. Communion between two people takes place only when there is a relationship in which both of them are deeply, intensely involved at the same time in the problem. Then there is not only verbal but nonverbal communication. And that is what we have to do here now.

So the mind sees that the whole content of my existence, my awareness, my conflict, is within this field of time, of thought, memories, experience, and knowledge, all of which is within the field of consciousness. That is, that all the religious images, the propaganda of two thousand years of priests, or three or five thousand years in the East, make you believe in something, with the reading of the literature and all the rest of it, and all that is within this field of consciousness which is time and thought. As we have said, the content makes up consciousness. Without it there is no consciousness. And the content being fragmented, one fragment observes the various other fragments, and tries to control or shape them. That is what we are doing all the time. One fragment calling itself virtuous, noble, religious, scientific, modern, whatever it is, trying to shape, dominate, suppress other fragments within the field of time, which is our consciousness. Are we meeting each other?

So my problem is—and it is your problem too—our problem is: how then can the mind observe nonfragmentarily, observe life as a total movement? Which means, can the mind be free of the content of consciousness?

Let's approach it differently. What is love? Is love pleasure? Is love desire? Is love the pursuit of a pleasure tasted yesterday and the demanding of it again, sexually or otherwise? Is that love? Is love fear, jealousy, anxiety, attachment? That is what we consider love to be, don't we? No? Don't we consider that to be love?

(Audience responds, "No.")

Oh, ashamed, are we? That is what we call love, in which there is attachment, dependence, the sense of attachment that comes from loneliness, insufficiency in oneself, not being able to stand alone, therefore leaning, depending on somebody. We depend on the milkman, the railwayman, the policeman—I am not talking of that kind of dependence—but of psychological dependence with all its problems, the problems of image in relationship—the image that the mind has built about the other, and the attachment to that image, and the denial of one image and the creating of another one. All that is what we call love. And the priests have invented another thing, the love of God, because it is much easier to love God, an image, an idea, a symbol, created by the mind or by the hand, than to find out what love is in relationship.

So what is love? And it is part of our consciousness. This thing called love in which there is the "me" and the "you." The "me" attached to you, possessing, dominating you, or you attached to me, possessing, dominating me. You satisfy my physical, sexual demands, and I satisfy you economically and so on. All that is what we call love; it is part of our consciousness. And is that love? The romantic love, the physical love, the love of one's country, for which you are willing to kill others, maim, destroy yourself, is that what love is? Obviously love is not emotionalism, sentimentality, the sloppy acceptance of, you know, "I love you and you love me." And talking about the beauty of love, the beautiful people. Is all that love?

Is love the product of thought? And it is, as we know it, because you have given me pleasure, physically, sexually, psychologically, and I love you because I can't live without you, I must possess you legally, morally, ethically you must be mine. And if you turn your face away, I am lost, I get anxious, jealous, angry, bitter, hateful. That is what we call love. And what are we going to do about all that? Just sit and listen? And you have done that for centuries, just sat and listened, or read about it, or some priest has talked about it, given you a thousand explanations. So is that love? And can the mind, the mind being the fragmented consciousness and its content, can that mind put away all these things? Totally deny all that, the dependency, the pursuit of pleasure, to be able to stand completely alone and understand what it means to be lonely, and not move away, run away from this loneliness? Can the mind in observing that, observe not verbally, but actually look, so that the very act of looking denies the whole thing?

So can the mind observe the content of consciousness without the movement of time? Do you understand? We said time is thought, of course. Whether that thought is the outcome of memories, experience, knowledge—obviously, which it is—whether that thought projects itself into a fantasy, some illusion, some future image, it is still part of time. So can the mind observe this thing called love as it is, not as it should be, which is also within the field of what is known as love? Can there be observation without the movement of thought which is time? And that observation demands tremendous attention, otherwise you can't do it.

Again let's look at this from a different point of view. Death comes to all of us, the young, the old, the middle-aged. It is inevitable, either through accident or old age, with disease, discomfort, pain, agony, and the doctors giving you medicine to keep you alive endlessly—I don't know for what purpose. There is death. Death being the ending of the brain with all its stored-up memories, experience, knowledge: of the brain that has sought security, shelter, in the "me," which is a series of symbols, ideas, words; that has sought security in some neurotic action and feels safe in it; that has sought security in a belief, I am a Christian, I believe in God or I believe in the Savior; or like the Communist and so on, that has sought security in a belief, an ideology which brings about all kinds of neurotic activity. That brain with all its consciousness dies, comes to an end.

Man has been frightened of that. And the Christians have taken comfort in the idea of resurrection and the Hindus and Buddhists in a future life. Future life of what? The resurrected, the future, what is that? This consciousness with all its content has died, and there is this hope, desire, seeking for comfort in a future life. Still within this field of consciousness. Are you following all this? I don't know why I put so much passion into all this, but it is my life—while I am living, I know I am going to die, I have rationalized it, looked at it, seen dead bodies being carried away, seen them buried, burned, or cremated, and the image has built round them. I have seen all that going on around me. And I am frightened, and being frightened, I must seek comfort, security, some kind of hope, and that is still within the field of my consciousness, of the living consciousness.

And when the brain through disease, accident, old age, comes to an end, what takes place? The mind is fully aware that consciousness is its content, there is no consciousness when there is no content. And when the brain dies, the content dies, obviously. The "me," which has been put together by thought, the "me" which is the image that thought has built through environment, through fear, through pleasure, through accident, through various forms of stimulation and demands, that "me" is the content and that content is my consciousness. That consciousness—the whole movement of memory, knowledge, experience—comes to an end at death. I may rationalize it, take comfort in rationalization, or take comfort in some ideology, belief, dogma, superstition, but that is not real, that is nothing to do with reality, whether all the religions proclaim there is this or there is not, that has nothing whatever to do with reality because that is mere say-so, the hear-say of somebody else. The mind has to find out for itself. So can the mind, living every day in an everyday relationship, live without the content that has made up the consciousness, which is essentially the "me" and its activity? And what takes place when the mind, the brain, the organism actually, not theoretically, actually comes to an end? This has been a problem for man, he has accumulated so much, he has acquired so much knowledge, so much information about so many things, and at the end of it all there is that thing called death. And as he cannot solve it—at least he hasn't been able to solve it—he has all the comforting images, speculations, beliefs: I will live, or I will not live. And if you do live with all these things, the consciousness carries on with its own content, which becomes the stream in which man is caught—that is a different matter, which we won't go into, because that involves another inquiry.

So what takes place when living now, today, this morning, the brain actually ceases, ends its memories, its images, its conclusions? Which means the content of consciousness. Can my brain, my consciousness, which is the "me," with all its content, can that come to an end, while living, not at the end of another ten years through disease, but while living now? Can that mind, can that consciousness empty its content, therefore empty the "me"? Do you understand all this? Is that ever possible? I get up and go to my room, after I have talked here. The knowledge where that room is must exist, otherwise it is not possible to live at all. That is clear.

So knowledge, which is based on experience and memory—from which all thought arises, and is therefore never free and never new—that knowledge must exist. It is part of consciousness, isn't it? Are you meeting all this? Somebody come with me. Riding a bicycle, driving a car, speaking a different language, that knowledge must exist, that is also part of consciousness. But that knowledge is used by the "me" as a separative movement, it uses that knowledge for its own psychological comfort and power, position, prestige, and all the rest of it. So I am asking myself whether that consciousness, with all its content as the psychological movement as the "me," can end now, so that the mind is aware of what death means, and see what happens.

When you actually die—I hope you won't die soon—when you die, this is what is going to happen, isn't it? Your heart will cease to beat and therefore to send blood to the brain, and the brain can survive for only three and a half or two minutes or whatever it is without fresh blood, and therefore it comes to an end. And the brain cells contain all your past activity, your consciousness, your desires, your memories, your hurts, your anxieties, all that is there, and that comes to an end. Now can all that come to an end, now, today, while living? If it does, then what takes place? The question may be unnecessary, or put to a mind that has never asked it and is merely afraid of coming to an end. But a mind that is not frightened, a mind that is not seeking or pursuing pleasure—which doesn't mean you can't enjoy the beauty of sunlight, the movement of leaves, the curve of a branch, or look at a beautiful this or that, which is real enjoyment—but can that mind observe the whole of the "me" with its content and end it?

Is that then immortality? Usually, the mortal is made into the immortal. The mortal dies, and immortality is an idea of the mortal who is the content of consciousness. So man has sought immortality in his books, his poems, his pictures, in the expression of his desires and their fulfillment. He has sought immortality in his family, his name. All that is still part of this consciousness with its content in time, and not therefore the timeless mind that sees immortality. So what happens to a mind, to a being, whose content of consciousness dies while living? Put that question to yourself seriously, take time to meditate, to go into it, not looking for a quick or some superficial, silly answer.

One has always observed as an observer who is different from the observed. The observer is a part of consciousness, with its content, observing another part of that consciousness, so there is a division between the observer and the observed. But the observer is within the field of that consciousness. And when it is seen that the observer is the observed, which is a fact, then is the content of consciousness in which there is no observer different from that which is observed? Because this is very important to ask and find out. The observer is the content of consciousness. And the observer separates himself from the observed, which is also part of that consciousness. Therefore, the division is unreal, it is artificial. And when you see that the observer is the observed, the mind totally ends all conflict.

Look, make it very simple. All relationship is based on the image that you have built about another and the other has built about you. And these two images have relationships, and these images are the result of many years of memories, experiences, knowledge, which you have built about her, and she has built about you. That is part of your consciousness. And what is the relationship when there is no image at all between you and her, and she has no image about you? Are you—if I may ask—are you aware that you have an image about him, to which you are dreadfully attached? And are you aware that you have an image about her to which you cling? Are you aware of this, conscious of it? And if you are conscious of it, do you see that your relationship with her, or hers to you, is based on that image, on those images? Can those images come to an end?

Then what is relationship? If the image has come to an end, which is the content of consciousness, which makes up your consciousness, the various images you have about yourself, about everything, when those images come to an end, then what is the relationship between you and her? Then is there an observer observing apart from the observed? Or is it a total movement of love in relationship? So love is a movement in relationship in which the observer is not.

So the mind—we are using the word *mind* here to include the brain, the physical organism, the totality—that mind has lived within the field of fragmentation, which makes up its consciousness, and without that content the observer is not. And when the observer is not, then relationship is not within the field of time which comes about when there is the image you have about her and she has about you. Can that image come to an end as you live daily? If that image doesn't come to an end, there is no love. It is then one fragment against another fragment. Now that you have heard that, don't draw a conclusion from it, see the truth of it—and you cannot see the truth of it verbally. You can hear the meaning of the words, but you have to see the significance of it, have an insight into it, see the truth of it, actually "what is."

One's Perception of Life Is Shaped by Concepts Already Established in One's Mind

———

WE ACCEPT SLOGANS, CLICHÉS, worn-out theories, or we invent new theories, new systems, but always within the field of consciousness which man has borne throughout the centuries. And consciousness is its content. Without its content there is no consciousness, as we know it. Please, as we have said, we are investigating these problems together. Therefore, you must partake, share, be involved in the investigation. You must not merely listen to the speaker, accepting or rejecting what he says, but together in fellowship, in cooperation, try to find out what the world around us and what the world inside us is like—whether there is a relationship between the inner and the outer. Or are they one, indivisible? And that is our concern. We must be committed to the understanding of this. And that is why we must not be led, but investigate together, so that there is no authority, there is no leader. To investigate, you must be totally concerned, not concerned one day and the rest of the time forget it. You must be concerned day after day, month after month, year after year, all your life—because this is your life.

So where do we find the answer, the logical, sane, healthy answer to all the problems? Not only the problems that lie outside

us, the wars, the violence, the cunning politicians, the prepara-
tions for war while talking of peace—you know what is happening around us, it is wicked, diabolical, appalling—but also the
problem of our relationship to that. We have to find out what our
place is in all this, our responsibility. To be responsible means to
respond adequately or totally to what is happening; and to respond to it, we must be deadly serious, right through our life.
That is why, if you are going to share what the speaker is saying,
you have to listen, to find out. To find out, not merely what the
speaker is saying, but to find out the right answer for yourself. You
must put aside your prejudices, nationalities, beliefs, experiences,
knowledge, hopes, everything, to find out. And that demands tremendous seriousness.

I do not think most of us realize what is actually going on in
the world. We read newspapers, watch television, go to political
or religious lectures, but all they give are superficial explanations.
But if one can go beyond that, put all that aside and observe
rather closely, one can see how man is deteriorating, degenerat-
ing. This degeneration takes place when one depends totally on
the outer, that is, when matter, the material, has become all-
important. When you look at all this, the divergence of opinions,
the ideologies, the political systems of right, left, or center, with
everybody talking of arranging, or trying to reform institutions,
government, you see that it is all still action in the field of time,
of thought and matter.

I am using words which are very simple, not some special jargon or terms that have a subtle or hidden meaning, but words as
they exist in the dictionary. To communicate, we must use simple,
clear language. And in communication, we must find out not only
the meaning of the words, but also the meaning that lies behind
them. Only then is there communication between the speaker
and you. But if you are merely caught in words and their verbal,
semantic meaning, then you will miss what lies behind them. To
communicate requires a great deal of concern on both sides, a
great deal of serious attention.

When one sees what is happening, when one observes the
politicians, the religious people, the various sects and denomina-
tions, one sees that they are concerned merely with the operation

of thought. Thought has created this world, the world of politics, economics, business, of social morality and the whole of the religious structure—whether in India, here, or anywhere—and it is all based on thought, whether it is Jewish thought, Arabic thought, Christian thought, or Hindu thought; it is all essentially the operation of thought as matter.

When you meditate, you are still caught within the pattern of that thought, still within that area of consciousness which is put together by thought. And when you try to find political answers, it is still within that area. All our problems, all our desires to find answers to those problems, are within that consciousness. If you have talked to any serious politicians, you will have seen, as the speaker has, in India, in America, here, and elsewhere, that they are all trying to find an answer, a political philosophy, a reformation of institutions within the field that thought has created.

So thought is trying to find an answer to that which it has created, an answer to the mess it has made in our personal relationships, in our relationship with the community, with the government. Politics, unfortunately, play a very important part in our social, moral, and environmental conditioning, and the politicians too—if they are at all serious—are trying to find an answer to these problems in the field, or through the function, of thought. That is so. I am not inventing this, it is not what I think, it is a fact. Thought has separated the world into the Americans, the Communists, the Socialists, the Germans, the Swiss, the Hindus, the Buddhists, and all the other religious divisions.

So is there an answer to all these problems through the operation of thought? Even your meditations, even your gods, your Christs and your Buddhas and all the rest, are the creations of thought, thought which is matter, which can only operate within the field of time. But if thought will give no answer to all these problems, then what will? That is what we are going to investigate.

We think that through thought, will, ambition, drive, and aggression we can solve all these problems, the problems of personal relationship between you and another, and religious problems by the introduction of "new" religions based on old traditions which, already dead in India, are brought over here or to America by gurus who are themselves soaked in tradition.

What is consciousness? What is the operation of thought? Thought has created everything around us, the whole technological field with all its scientific knowledge and the culture in which we live: the Christian culture, the Western culture, or the Eastern culture—they are all put together by thought. The gods, the saviors—our thought has created them. God has not created us in his image; we have created God in our image, and we pursue that image which thought has created and we call that religious activity.

When one says, "I am conscious," it implies that I am as much as possible conscious of everything happening around me and, further, it means I am aware of what is happening within that consciousness. The investigation of the content of consciousness implies also what lies beyond—if there is something beyond the so-called consciousness. All your meditations are in that area, all your pursuits of pleasure, fear, greed, envy, brutality, violence, are within that field. And thought is always endeavoring to go beyond it, asserting the ineffable, the unnamable, the unknowable, and so on.

The content of consciousness is consciousness. Your consciousness, or another's consciousness, is its content. If it is born in India, then all the traditions, superstitions, hopes, fears, sorrows, anxieties, violence, sexual demands, aggression, the beliefs, dogmas, and creeds of that country are the content of its consciousness. Yet the content of consciousness is extraordinarily similar, whether one is born in the East or in the West.

Consider, look at, your own consciousness, if you can. You are brought up in a religious culture as a Christian, believing in saviors, rituals, creeds, and dogmas on the one hand and social immorality, accepting wars, nationalities and their division, and therefore restricting economic expansion and consideration for others, on the other. Your personal unhappiness, ambitions, fears, greeds, aggressiveness, demands, loneliness, sorrow, your lack of relationship with another, isolation, frustration, confusion, misery, all that is consciousness, whether you are of the East or the West. With variations, with joys, with more knowledge or with less knowledge, all that is the content of your consciousness.

Without that content there is no consciousness as we know it.

All education in the schools, the colleges, the universities, is based on the acquiring of more knowledge, more information, but functioning always within this area. Any political reform, based on a new political philosophy, having dropped Marxism or some other established philosophy, is an invention still within that area. And so man goes on suffering, unhappy, lonely, fearful of death and of living, hoping for some great leader to come and take him out of his misery—a new savior, a new politician. In this confusion we are so irresponsible, because out of our own disorder we are going to create tyrants, hoping they will create order within this area. This is what is happening outside us and inside us.

So what shall we do? Not what will the politicians do, because they are as confused, unhappy, ambitious, envious as we are. Any leader we choose will be like us; we will not choose a leader who is totally different from us. So that is the actual picture of our life: conflict, inside and outside, struggle, one opposed to the other, appalling selfishness—you know the whole picture.

The first thing that behooves one, if one is at all serious—and one must be serious when there is so much sorrow in the world—is to find out for oneself through careful, slow, patient, hesitant investigation whether there is any way of solving all these problems other than through the operation of thought. Is there an action which is not based on thought? Is there an intelligence which is not the function or result of thought, which is not put together by thought, which does not come about through cunning, through friction and struggle, but something entirely different? That is what I want to communicate. Therefore, one has to listen not just to the speaker—but to the very action of listening. How does one listen? Does one ever really listen at all? Is one free to listen, or does one always listen with the cunning operations of thought, with interpretation, or prejudice? One has to listen, if one is free, to the content of one's consciousness. Listen, not only to what is at the surface, which is fairly simple, but to the deeper layers. That means listen to the totality of consciousness.

So from that arises the question: how does one listen to and look at one's consciousness? The speaker was born in a country where, as a Brahmin, one absorbed all the prejudices, irrationalities and superstitions, beliefs, class differences; the young mind absorbed it all, the tradition, the rituals, the extraordinary orthodoxy, and the tremendous discipline that group imposed upon itself. And then one moves to the West. Again he absorbs all that is there; the content of his consciousness is what has been put into it, what he has learned, what his thoughts are, and the thought which recognizes its own emotions and so on. That is the content and the consciousness of this person. Within that area he has all the problems—whether political, religious, personal, communal—all the problems are there. And not being able to solve them himself, he looks to books, to others, asking: "Please tell me what to do, how to meditate, what shall I do about my personal relationship with my wife, or my girlfriend or whoever it is, between myself and my parents, should I believe in Jesus or the Buddha, or the new guru who comes along with a lot of nonsense?"—searching for a new philosophy of life, a new philosophy of politics, and so on, all within this area. And man has done this from time immemorial.

There is no answer within that area. You may meditate for hours, sitting in a certain posture, breathing in a special way, but it is still within that area because you want something out of meditation. I do not know if you see all this. So there is this content of consciousness, dull, stupid, traditional thought, recognizing all its emotions—otherwise they are not emotions—always it is thought, which is the response of memory, knowledge, and experience, that is operating. Now can the mind look at this? Can you look at the operation of thought? And when you look, who is the observer who is looking at the content, is it different from the content? This is really a very important question to ask and to find an answer to. Is the observer different from the content and therefore capable of changing, altering, and going beyond the content? Or is it that the observer is the same as the content?

First look. If the observer—the "I" that looks, the "me" that looks—is different from the observed, then there is a division between the observer and the observed, therefore conflict. I must not do this, I should do that—I must get rid of my particular prejudice and adopt a new prejudice—get rid of my old gods and take on new gods. So when there is a division between the observer and the observed, there must be conflict. That is a principle, that is a law. So do I observe the content of my consciousness as if I were an outsider looking in, altering the pieces, and moving the pieces to different places? Or am I, the observer, the thinker, the experiencer, the same as that thought which is observed, experienced, seen?

If I look at the content of my consciousness as an outsider observing, then there must be conflict between what is observed and the observer. So what happens when I hear this statement that when there is a division between the observer and the observed, there is conflict? There must be conflict in that division, and in that conflict we have lived, the "me" and the "not me," "we" and "they." If "I," the observer, am different from anger, I try to control it, suppress it, dominate it, overcome it, and all the rest, and there is conflict. But is the observer different at all; or is he essentially the same as the observed? If he is the same, then there is no conflict, is there? The understanding of that is intelligence. Then intelligence operates and not conflict.

It would be a thousand pities if you did not understand this simple thing. Man has lived in conflict and he wants peace, and there can never be peace through conflict. However much armament you have against the equally powerful armament of another, there will never be peace. Only when intelligence operates will there be peace, intelligence which comes when one understands that there is no division between the observer and the observed. The insight into that very fact, that very truth, brings this intelligence. Have you got it? This is a very serious thing, for then you will see you have no nationality—you may have a passport, but you have no nationality—you have no gods, there is no outside authority nor inward authority. The only authority then is intelligence, but not the cunning intelligence of thought, which is mere knowledge operating within a certain area—that is not intelligence.

So this is the first thing to understand when you look at your consciousness: this division between the thinker and the thought, between the observer and the observed, between the experiencer and the experienced, is false, for they are one. There is no thinker if you do not think. Thought has created the thinker. So that is the first thing to understand, to have an insight into the truth of it, the fact of it, as palpable as you are sitting here, so that there is no conflict between the observer and the observed.

So what is the content of your consciousness, the hidden as well as the open? Can you look at it? But do not make an effort. This you can find out, not just sitting here but in your relationships. That is the mirror in which you will see. Not by closing your eyes, or by going off into the woods and thinking up some dreams, but in the actual fact of relationship between man and woman, with your neighbor, your politician, your gods, your gurus, you will observe your reactions, attitudes, prejudices, images, your constant groping, and all the rest—it is in that. What you are doing now is merely ploughing, and we can go on ploughing, ploughing, ploughing and never sowing. You can only sow when you observe your relationships and see what is actually taking place.

From listening you move to looking. And you can look as much as you like and begin to distinguish various qualities and tendencies and so on, but if you look as an observer different from the observed, then you are bound to create conflict, therefore further suffering. When you have the insight, the truth of this, that the observer is the observed, then conflict ceases altogether. Then a totally different kind of energy comes into operation. There are different kinds of energy: physical energy, from good food; there may be energy created by emotionalism, sentimentality; there is energy created by thought through various conflicts and tensions; within that field of energy we have lived. And we are still trying to find greater energy within that field, to solve our problems, which needs tremendous energy. But there is a different kind of energy, or the continuation of this energy in a totally different form, when the mind is operating completely, not in the field of thought, but intelligently.

Can the mind observe its content without any choice as to the content—not choosing any part of the content, any part of the piece, but observing totally? Now, how is it possible to observe totally? When I look at a map of France, as I come from England and cross the Channel, I see the road leading to Gstaad. I can tell the mileage, I can see the direction, and that is very simple because it is marked on the map and I follow it. In doing that, I do not look at any other part of the map because I know the direction in which I want to go to, so that that direction excludes all others.

In the same way, a mind that is seeking in a given direction does not see the whole. If I want to find something, something which I think is real, then the direction is set and I follow that direction and my mind is incapable of seeing the totality. Now, when I look at the content of my consciousness—which is the same as yours—I have set a direction to go beyond it. A movement in a particular direction, seeking a certain pleasure, not wanting to do this or that, makes one incapable of seeing the whole. If I am a scientist, I see only in a certain direction. If I am an artist, there again, if I have a certain talent or gift, I see only in a certain direction. But if there is a movement in a particular direction, the mind is incapable of seeing the totality and the immensity of that totality.

So can the mind have no direction at all? This is a difficult question—please listen to it. Of course the mind has to have a direction when I go from here to the house, or when I have to drive a car, when I have to do some technical function—those are all directions. But I am talking of a mind that understands the nature of direction and is therefore capable of seeing the whole. When it sees the whole, it can then also operate in direction.

I wonder if you get this? If I have the whole picture in mind, then I can take in the detail. But if my mind operates only in a detail, then I cannot take in the whole. If I am concerned with my opinions, my anxieties, with what I want to do, with what I must do, I cannot see the whole—obviously. If I come from India with my prejudices, superstitions, and traditions, I cannot see the whole. So my question is: can the mind be free of direction?— which does not mean that it is without direction. When it operates from the whole, the direction becomes clear, very strong, and effective. But when the mind operates only in a direction according to the pattern it has set for itself, then it cannot see the whole.

There is the content of my consciousness—the content makes my consciousness. Now, can I look at it as a whole? Without any direction, without any judgment, without any choice, just look, which implies no observer at all, for that observer is the past—can it look with that intelligence which is not put together by thought, for thought is the past? Do it—it requires tremendous discipline; not the discipline of suppression, control, imitation, or conformity, but a discipline that is an act in which the truth is seen. The operation of truth creates its own action, which is discipline.

Can your mind look at its content, when you talk to another, in your gestures, in the way you walk, in the way you sit and eat, in the way you behave? Behavior indicates the content of your consciousness—whether you are behaving according to pleasure, reward, or pain, which are part of your consciousness. The psychologists are saying that, so far, man has been educated on the principle of reward and punishment, heaven and hell. Now they say he must be educated on the principle of reward. Do not punish him but reward him—which is the same thing. They go from one thing to another, thinking they are solving everything. To see the absurdity of reward and punishment is to see the whole. When you see the whole, there is the operation of intelligence, which functions when you behave. You are not then behaving according to reward or punishment.

Behavior exposes the content of your consciousness. You may hide yourself behind polished, very carefully drilled behavior, but such behavior is merely mechanical. From that arises another question. Is the mind entirely mechanical? Or is there any portion of the brain where it is not mechanical at all?

I will go over what has already been said. Outside of us, in the political world, with its new political philosophies, and in the economic, the religious, or the social world, and so on, man is searching, searching. There are new gods, new gurus, new leaders. And when you observe all this very clearly, you see that man is functioning within the field of thought. Thought is essentially never free, thought is always old, because thought is the response of memory as knowledge and experience. Thought is matter, it is of the material world. And thought is trying to escape from that material world into a nonmaterial world, and trying to escape into the nonmaterial world by thought is still a material process.

We have all the moral, social, and economic problems of the individual and the collective. The individual is essentially, intrinsically, part of the collective. The individual is different from the collective in that he may have different tendencies, a different occupation, different moods, and so on, but he is intrinsically part of the culture, which is society. Now, those are facts as to what is going on about us. The facts as to what is going on inside us are very much the same. We are trying to find an answer to the major problems of our human life through the operation of thought—thought which the Greeks imposed upon the West, with their political philosophy, their mathematics, and so on. Thought has not found an answer, and it never will. So we must go then into the whole structure of thought and the content which it has created as consciousness. We must then observe the operation of thought in relationship, in our daily life. That observation implies having an insight as to whether it is a fact that the observer is different from the observed, for if there is a difference, there must inevitably be conflict, just as there is between two ideologies—two ideologies which are the inventions of thought, conditioned by the culture in which they have developed.

Now can you, in your daily life, observe this? In such observation you will find out what your behavior is, whether it is based on the principle of reward and punishment—as most of our behavior is, however polished and refined. From that observation one begins to learn what real intelligence is. Not the intelligence obtained from a book, or from experience; that is not intelligence at all. Intelligence has nothing whatsoever to do with thought. Intelligence operates when the mind sees the whole, the endless whole, not my country, my problems, my little gods, my meditations, whether this is right or this is wrong. It sees the whole implication of living. And this quality of intelligence has its own tremendous energy.

One's Uniqueness as a Human Being Lies in Complete Freedom from the Content of One's Consciousness

---

THE QUESTION IS: CAN the content of consciousness, which makes up consciousness as we know it, be completely emptied? Is this all Greek? Are we following each other? The whole inward content of consciousness is what it has thought, what it has accumulated, what it has received through tradition, culture, struggle, pain, sorrow, deception. Without that content, what is consciousness? I only know my consciousness because of its content. I am a Hindu, Buddhist, Christian, Catholic, Communist, Socialist, an artist, a scientist, a philosopher. I am attached to this house, she is my wife, you are my friend, the images, the conclusions, the remembrances that I have built through forty, fifty, a hundred years are the content.

That content is my consciousness, as yours is yours. And that area of consciousness is time, because it is the area of thought, of measurement—of comparing, evaluating, judging—it is within that area. Within that area are all my conscious or unconscious thoughts. And any movement within that area is within the movement of consciousness-with-its-content. Therefore, space in this consciousness-with-its-content is very limited. Please, let us learn this together. If we learn this together, it will be yours, not mine. Then you are free of all leaders, free of all teaching; it will be your mind learning, therefore there is energy, you will be passionate to find out. But if you are following somebody like a dog, then you lose all energy.

As we have said, within the area of consciousness-with-its-content, which is time, space is very small. You can expand the space by imagination, by contrivance, extending it by various processes, by thinking more, more subtly, more deliberately, but it is still within the limited space of consciousness-with-its-content. Are you getting it?

So any movement to go beyond itself is still within the content. That is why when you take drugs of any kind, LSD, marijuana, opium, and so forth, it is still the activity of thought within that consciousness; and when you think you are going beyond it, you are still within it. It is only an idea, or you experience more deeply the content. So one sees that, however expanded, space in the content—which is the "me," the ego, the person, the so-called individual—within that consciousness must always be limited. So to consciously make an effort to reach something beyond itself invites illusion—I wonder if you understand this? And to be told by a guru that you will find it, without understanding and emptying all that content, is so absurd; while merely to practice in order to get something is like the blind leading the blind, and generally the gurus are blind, and so are the followers.

So that is the question: mind is its content; the brain is the past, and from that past thought functions, and thought is never free and never new. So the question arises: how can that content be emptied? Not by a method, because the moment you practice a method, somebody has given it to you, or you invent your own and that becomes mechanical, and therefore, it is still within the field of time and limited space.

I do not know if you have ever thought or gone into yourself to find out what space is—not space or time or timelessness according to science fiction, but to inquire, to learn what space is. We are going to do this. Can the mind see its own limitation? And the very perception of that limitation is the ending of that limitation. Not how to empty the mind, but to see the content that makes up consciousness, to see that totally, and to perceive, listen to all the movement of that consciousness—and the very perception of it is the ending of it, not how to end it. If I see something false, the very perception of the false is the true. The very perception of my telling a lie is the truth. The very perception of my envy is the freedom from envy, is the truth. That is, you can see very clearly, observe very clearly only when there is no observer—the observer being the past, the image, the conclusion, the opinion, the judgment. So can the mind see clearly without any effort its content, and the limitation of it, which means the lack of space, and the time-binding quality of consciousness-with-its-content?

Can you see this? And you can see the totality of it, both the unconscious content as well as the conscious content, only when you can look silently, when the observer is totally silent. That is, if I want to see you, my vision mustn't be blurred; I must have very good eyesight to see the whole outline of you, the hair, the bone structure of your face, and so on; I must look very clearly. That means there must be attention, and in that attention there is energy. Whereas when you make an effort to be attentive, that effort is a wastage of energy. When you try to control, that is a wastage of energy—control implies conformity, comparison, suppression—all that is a wastage of energy. When there is perception, there is attention, which is total energy, in which there is not a breath of wastage of energy.

Now when you look with energy, at the whole conscious as well as the unconscious content, the mind then is empty. This is not an illusion of mine, this is not what I think, or the conclusion I have come to. If I have a conclusion, if I think this is right, then I am in illusion. And knowing it to be an illusion, I wouldn't talk. Because then it is like the blind leading the blind. But you can see for yourself the logic, the sanity of it. That is, if you are listening, if you are paying attention, if you really want to find out. That is, whether it is possible for the unconscious-with-its-content to expose totally all its depth.

First see the question and then proceed from there. Like everything else in life, we have divided consciousness—into the conscious and the unconscious—like the artist and the businessman; this division, this fragmentation exists, induced by our culture, by our education. And you are asking a question, which is: there is this division between conscious and unconscious and the unconscious has its motives, its racial inheritance, its experience, and so on—how can all that be exposed to the light of intelligence, to the light of perception? Do you ask this question? If you ask this question, are you asking it as an analyzer who is going to analyze the content and therefore the division, contradiction, conflict, sorrow, and all the rest of it? Or are you asking this question not knowing the answer? Because this is important. If you are saying I honestly, seriously don't know how to expose this whole hidden structure of consciousness, I really don't know, then when you approach it not knowing, you are going to learn. But if you have any kind of conclusion, opinion, for or against, that it cannot be, that it can be, then you are approaching it with a mind that has already assumed the answer or no answer.

Therefore, when a mind says, "I do not know," this is the truth, this is honesty—you may know according to some philosopher, psychologist, or analyst, but it is not *your* knowing—it is *their* knowing and you interpret that and try to understand them, not what is actual. So when you say, "I do not know," what is there then? Have you understood? When you say, "I do not know," the content has no importance whatsoever. Oh, do see this. Because the mind is then a fresh mind—you understand? It is the new mind that says "I don't know." When you say this, not just verbally for amusement, but with depth, with meaning, with honesty, that state of mind that does not know is consciousness empty of its content. It is the knowing that is the content. Have you got it? Do you see it?

So the mind can never say it knows. Therefore, it is always new, living, acting; therefore, it has no anchorage. It is only when it is anchored that it gathers opinions, conclusions, and separation. Now this is meditation. Which is, meditation is to perceive the truth each second—not the truth ultimately. To perceive the true and the false each second. To perceive the truth that the content is consciousness. To see the truth that I do not know how to deal with this thing. That is the truth, not knowing; therefore, not knowing is the state in which there is no content. It is so terribly simple—that is what you are objecting to! You want something clever, complicated, contrived, and you object to seeing something extraordinarily simple, and therefore extraordinarily beautiful!

So can the mind, which is the brain, see its own limitation, which is the bondage of time and the limitation of space? And as long as one lives within that limited space and time-binding movement, there must be suffering, there must be psychological despair, hope and anxiety, all that. So when the mind has perceived the truth of this, then what is time? Is there then a different dimension which thought cannot touch, therefore cannot describe? We have said thought is measure and therefore time. We live by measurement, all our structure of thinking is based on measurement, which is comparison, evaluation, becoming. And thought as measurement tries to go beyond itself and discover for itself if there is something immeasurable. And to see the falseness of that is the truth. I wonder if you see this? The truth is to see the false, and the false is when thought seeks that which is not measurable, which is not of time, which is not of that limited space which is the content of consciousness.

Choiceless Awareness

───

CHOICELESS AWARENESS IMPLIES TO be aware both objectively, outside, and inwardly, without any choice. Just to be aware of the colors, of this tent, of the trees, the mountains, nature—just to be aware. Not choose, say "I like this," "I don't like that," or "I want this," "I don't want that." To observe without the observer. The observer is the past, who is conditioned; therefore, he is always looking from that conditioned point of view, so there is like and dislike, my race, your race, my God, your God, and all the rest of it. We are saying to be aware implies to observe the whole environment around you, the mountains, the trees, the ugly wars, the towns, to be aware, to look at it. And in that observation there is no decision, no will, no choice.

Freedom Is Found in the Choiceless Awareness of Daily Existence and Activity

———

I T IS REALLY A very important subject and needs a great deal of exploration, of inquiry to find out whether the mind can ever be free or is always time-bound. Is it possible for the mind, living in this world, functioning as it must with all the daily problems—with the many conflicting desires, opposing elements, influences, and various contradictions that one lives in, with all the tortures and passing joys—can such a mind ever be free, not only superficially but profoundly, at the very root of its existence? And so we have asked this question, whether man living in this extraordinarily complex society, where he has to earn a livelihood, perhaps have a family, live in competition and acquisition, whether he can go beyond all that, not into abstraction, not into an idea or formula, or a concept of freedom, but actually be free.

"Freedom from" is an abstraction, but freedom is in observing "what is" and going beyond it. Do not be puzzled. But first, if I may suggest, just listen, not accepting or denying, just have the sensitivity to listen, without drawing any conclusion, reacting defensively or resisting or translating what we are saying into your own, particular language. Listen as you listen to those crows—which are noisy, flying about, trying to find a tree for the night where they will be unmolested—and be quiet. You listen, and you cannot do anything about it, you cannot ask them to stop calling to each other. You just listen. But if you resist the noise they make, that very resistance denies the freedom to listen to the crows. And if you resist, because you say "I want to listen to what is being said and they are making an awful lot of noise," that very resistance is an act that prevents you from listening and therefore denies the freedom to listen.

Now, if you will, listen not just to the word or its meaning, but try to comprehend the whole inwardness of this word *freedom*. That is, we are together going to share this question, travel together, investigate together, understand together what this freedom implies, whether a mind—that is, your mind—that has been nurtured in time, a brain that has evolved through time, that has accumulated thousands of experiences, that has been conditioned in various cultures, whether such a mind can be free—not in some utopian, religious sense of freedom, but actually living in this confused and contradictory world.

We are going to ask whether this mind, your mind, as you know it, as you have observed it, whether it can ever, both on the surface and deeply inwardly, be completely free. Because if we do not answer this question for ourselves, we shall always be living in the prison of time, time being the past, time being thought, time being sorrow. And unless we really see the truth of this, we shall always live in conflict, in sorrow, the prison of thought. I do not know how you regard this question, not what your religious teachers have said, not the Gita, the Upanishads, your gurus, your social structure, your economic condition, but what you think, what you say, which is far more important than all the books put together. It means that you have to find the truth of this yourself. Never repeat what others have said but first find out for yourself, test it out for yourself, testing what you think, what you see, not test what others have said. Therefore, you are free from authority.

As I said, please listen. As you are listening, act, which means, as you listen, see the truth of it. We have to rely on scientific knowledge, other people's experiments, other people's accumulation of mathematical, geographical, scientific, biological knowledge. That is inevitable. If you want to be an engineer, you have to have the knowledge gathered by others about mathematics, structure, strain, and so on. But if you would find out for yourself what truth is—if there is such a thing—you cannot possibly accept the accumulated knowledge of what others have said, which is what you have done.

What matters is what you think, how you live. And to find out how you live, how you act, what you do, you have to discard totally all the knowledge of the experts and professionals who have instructed you how to live. Please do understand this. Freedom is not permissiveness; freedom is necessary for the human mind, so that it can function healthily, normally, sanely. As I said, freedom from something—like freedom from anger, jealousy, or aggression—is an abstraction and therefore not real. A man who says to himself "I must be free from anger or from jealousy" is not free; but the man who says "I must observe the fact of anger, actually what it is and learn the whole structure of anger," observing directly for himself, finds freedom through that observation, not through cultivation of the opposite. To cultivate bravery when one is not brave is not freedom, but to understand the nature and structure of cowardice and to remain with it, not trying to suppress it or go beyond it, but to remain with it, look at it, learn all about it, perceive the truth of it instantly, such a mind is free from cowardice and bravery. That is, direct perception is freedom, not the cultivation of the opposite. The cultivation of the opposite implies time.

Thought Is Time

W HEN THE MIND IS aware of disorder, out of that awareness is the flowering of order which is virtue, and when
that is really and deeply and honestly laid, then we can go into
the question of whether there is anything sacred. To come upon
that, you must investigate the nature of time and thought.

Because unless time has a stop, the mind cannot perceive anything sacred, anything new. So it is very important to inquire
whether thought has any relationship to time, and what time is.
Obviously there is time by the watch, today, yesterday, and tomorrow. Planning, going from here to there, planning to do
certain things. To learn a language, to learn how to drive a car,
to do any technological work, you must have time. All this is
meditation.

So what is time apart from chronological time? Time is movement psychologically, from here to there, as well as physically,
from here to that house. So the movement between this and that
is time. The space between this and that, the covering of that
space is time, the movement to that is time. So all movement is
time. Both physically, going from here to Paris, New York, or
wherever you will, requires time. And also to change psychologically "what is" into "what should be" requires time, its movement,
at least we think so. So time is movement in space, created by
thought as this and achieving that. Thought then is time, thought

is movement in time. Does this mean anything to any of you? Are we journeying together?

Please, this requires tremendous attention, care, a sense of the nonpersonal, nonpleasurable, where desire doesn't enter at all. That requires great care, and that care brings its own order, which is its own discipline. So thought is movement between "what is" and "what should be." Thought is time to cover that space, and as long as there is the division between this and that psychologically, there is the movement of thought in time. So thought is time as movement. And is there time as movement, thought, when there is only observation of "what is"?—which is observation, not as the observer and the observed but only observation, without the movement of going beyond "what is." It is very important for the mind to understand this, because thought can create the most marvelous images of that which is sacred and holy, which all religions have done. All religions are based on thought, on thought which has been organized into belief, dogma, rituals. So unless there is complete understanding of thought as time and movement, the mind cannot possibly go beyond itself.

As we said, we are trained, educated, drilled into changing "what is" into "what should be"—the ideal. And the word *ideal* comes from the word *idea*, which means to see, only that. Not draw an abstraction from what you see, but actually remain with what you see. So we are trained to change "what is" into "what should be." That training is the movement of thought to cover the space between "what is" and "what should be," and that takes time. That whole movement of thought in space is time necessary to change "what is" into "what should be."

But the observer is the observed; therefore, there is nothing to change. Because there is only "what is." The observer doesn't know what to do with "what is" and therefore tries various methods to change "what is," to control or suppress it. But the observer is the observed, the "what is" is the observer, as anger or jealousy is—jealousy is the observer, there isn't jealousy separate from the observer, both are one. So when there is no movement to change "what is"—movement as thought in time—when thought perceives that there is no possibility of changing "what is," then the "what is" ceases entirely because the observer is the observed. Go into this very deeply and you will see for yourself, it is really quite simple.

Say I dislike someone, and think the dislike is different from "me." The entity that dislikes is dislike itself, it is not separate, and when thought says "I must get over my dislike," then it is movement in time to get over that which actually is, which is created by thought. When it is seen that the observer, the entity, and the thing called dislike are the same, there is complete immobility, which is not "staticism," but complete motionlessness, therefore complete silence. Time as movement, time as thought achieving a result, comes totally to an end; therefore, action is instantaneous. So the mind has laid the foundation and is free from disorder. And on this basis there is therefore the flowering and beauty of virtue. And in that foundation is the relationship between you and another, in which there is no activity of image, there is only relationship, not the image adjusting itself to the other image. And there is only "what is" and not the changing of "what is." The changing of "what is," or transforming of "what is," is the movement of thought in time.

When you have come to that point, the mind and also the brain cells become totally still. The brain, which holds the memories, experience, knowledge, can and must function in the field of the known. But now that mind, that brain, is free from the activity of time and thought. Then the mind is completely still. All this takes place effortlessly, must take place without any sense of discipline, control, all that belongs to disorder. What we are saying is something totally different from what your gurus, "masters," Zen, all that, say. In this there is no authority, there is no following another. If you follow somebody, you not only destroy yourself but also the other. So for a religious mind there is no authority whatsoever. But it has got intelligence and applies that intelligence. There is the authority of the scientist, the doctor, the driving instructor. Otherwise, there is no authority, there is no guru.

Time Is the Psychological Enemy

―――――

W E HAVE ALREADY TALKED about the nature of time. Please don't get impatient, we must talk about it again. We said time is the past, time is the future, and that the future is now. The future is what you are now. If I am violent now and do not radically change now, the future is now. Have you understood this thing? We must share this together, it is not my truth or your truth, truth is not personal, has no path. And this is a fact, it is the truth that all time, the past, the future, and the present are contained in the now. It is logical, rational, it is intellectually irrefutable. But you may not like it. And most of us live in like and dislike; we don't want to actually face something, we would rather slur over things. As we are—I hope—serious people, let us look, even briefly, at this thing together: that time, the past, the present, and the future, are in the now.

Suppose one is self-centered, which becomes very, very limited. That self-centeredness may identify itself with something greater, but it will still be self-centeredness. If I identify myself with my country, my nation, my religion, my superstitions, and so on, that very identification is the continuation of self-centeredness. I have only used a different set of words, but essentially this identifying process is self-centeredness. Please, the speaker is not trying to convince you of anything. On the contrary, doubt, question, discuss, don't accept. But examine with a critical, sharp brain. The fact is, one lives in disorder. You can't deny it. You may cover it up, run away from it, but we human beings live in disorder, hating, loving, anxious, wanting security, knowing there is insecurity because we live constantly with the threat of war and also the threat of death. So we live in disorder. Will time solve that disorder? We have lived on this earth, archaeologists and biologists say, for some forty-five thousand years as human beings. And despite those long periods of evolution, we are now what we are, in conflict, in disorder.

Time, this long duration, has not solved the problem. So we may have misunderstood time. That is, we have hoped that with another forty thousand years, by acquiring a great deal of knowledge, ascending through knowledge, we will eventually come out without any conflict, any disorder. So by relying on time, we may have misunderstood its meaning. I have been this, or I am this, give me time to change. And we have had forty or fifty thousand years of time, and we are still very primitive. So that kind of thinking in time may be wrong. There may be a new way of looking at it, a new approach to this whole problem.

You need time to go from here to your house and so on, but psychologically—if you don't like psychologically, inwardly, or if you don't like that, inside the skin—we have accepted time as a duration from which we will eventually emerge as human beings who are extraordinarily sane, rational, healthy, without conflict. And time has not shown that. You have had forty thousand years, and if you wait another forty thousand years, you will be exactly the same. This is logical.

So let us look at the whole meaning of time. Time is the past, the whole content of our consciousness, and if you don't like the word *consciousness*, the whole world of reactions, which is the past—the past with all its inherited, acquired, racial, environmental memories which we have gathered for thousands of years. And that time, that past, is now. You are the past. Agreed? You are the past, you are all the accumulated memory of the past, you are memory. That memory needs time to accumulate. And the future, tomorrow, and a thousand tomorrows, is what you are now—clear? Obviously. So the future is now. And is it possible—please understand this—not to allow the old time to interfere but to allow this new sense of all time being now?

Do you understand this? Suppose I live in disorder, which I have become aware of. And I say to myself I will gradually work at it, think about it, go into it, which all means time, which is tomorrow. I will find out the cause of it. All that takes time. At least, please, agree to that, see that fact. And I see that this is a false way of approaching time. So I put it aside completely. Which means I am breaking—or rather seeing the fact is breaking—the conditioning of the brain, which has accepted the old pattern of time.

So as I have put aside the old way of thinking in terms of time, I now look at time as it is. All time is now. If that is seen, I change completely now, which is to uncondition the brain, which has been accustomed to the old approach to time, and I break that conditioning because I see the fact and falseness of it. And in that very perception there has been a radical change, which means that in the very perception there is instant action. I act without time, which means the thinking process doesn't take place. Do you get it? Oh, gosh!

It is very fascinating, this, if you go into it. Thought is time. Because thought is the accumulated response of memory. That memory has been accumulating through time; it is the outcome of knowledge. To accumulate knowledge, you need time, and knowledge comes from the accumulation of experience. Experience is limited, so knowledge is limited, and memory is limited, so thought is limited. Now I have said thought is time. And if we utilize time, which is thought, to change what I am now, it will be futile. But if I see—if there is perception, not I see—if there is perception of the fact that all time is contained in the now, then what takes place? You understand the proposition? I am violent, I live in disorder, and I perceive that disorder. And I also see the fact, the truth, that all time is now. And my perception of this must be so acute, so clear, and that clarity is not the product of time.

So we must discuss what is perception. What is it to see clearly?—not only ourselves as we are, but also to see clearly what is happening in the world. What is happening clearly in the world is the extension of division—nations, religions, sects, gurus, and so on, the whole lot of them may talk politically, religiously about peace and unity; they want us all to join their unity.

So outwardly there is this immense disorder, and the ultimate expression of that disorder is war, killing each other. And we also live in disorder. And that disorder is brought about through time; we have lived with it for centuries, so time in the old sense is not going to solve it. So what is perception? Can you see something very clearly if you have prejudice? Obviously not. If you are personal?—I get hurt, please don't say anything to me. My opinions are so strong, I have thought this out and I stick to what I have thought out. All these factors, which are personal—not objective, clear—prevent perception. It is like putting on tinted glasses. Or like photographic lenses that take the picture and record it on the film, but if the film is full, it cannot take any more pictures.

So what we do is retain, which means you can't see any more. But if instead you look and put it aside, you finish with it. That means you have to have a very clear, strong, active brain, so that there is no personal prejudice, no attachment to a thing. When there is such perception, that perception is not a factor of time, so that when there is disorder, you see it instantly, the cause, and all the division. There is the ending of it immediately, which means that it will not pop up again next day. When once you see a danger, a poisonous snake, you don't play with it. That is the end of it. But we don't see the danger because we are so prejudiced, we are so narrow-minded, full with our own concerns.

So disorder can only end now, not tomorrow. As you are sitting there, observe your own disorder, see whether you can see, perceive it clearly, with all its ramifications. When you perceive it completely, that is the end of it. And that perception is not possible if you are prejudiced, if you are personal.

We ought also to talk over together the question of fear. I am sure this will interest you. I know that what we have said you may consider to be very intellectual. I know you will say this. It is not intellectual. Intellect is necessary, as emotions are necessary, but when one predominates over the other, then the trouble begins.

So let us talk about fear and explore together what is its cause, its nature, whether it can end completely. Or must we carry on for the rest of human existence living in fear? If one is aware at all, conscious, we have many fears. Fear of darkness, fear of living, fear of public opinion, fear of what my neighbor might say, fear of my wife or husband or whoever, fear of insecurity, fear when you have economic security that you might lose it. Why haven't we solved these fears? You have dealt with the problem of war by continuing war, and you have applied your brain to preparing for war. All the generals are preparing for war, with plans, submarines, aircraft—all the rest of it.

They have exercised their brains to produce all that. Why haven't the same brains been applied to this enormous sense of fear man has had from the beginning of time? Which means why have you and the speaker not gone into this question seriously, as you do go very seriously when you are hungry or ambitious? When you want more money, then you work at it. The psychologists, the therapists, have explained the causes of fear in different ways. If we could put aside everything they have said, because after all it is all what they have said, it may be merely verbal. They might be as scared as you—probably they are! I have met several of them, I know they are scared like you, about something or other. And is it possible to end fear? Apply your feelings, your emotions, and your brain to work at this, not escaping from it, not trying to rationalize it, but see why we are incapable or have allowed ourselves to become incapable.

What is fear? You know when it is there, the nature of it, how it throbs, how your physical organism shrinks, how your brain becomes addled, almost paralyzed. Don't you know all this? It is a fact. It affects your sleep, your daily life, it brings suspicion, anxiety, depression, and you cling to something and hope that won't change and won't bring fear. Either we deal with the root of fear, or we trim its branches. Which do you want to do? There are a thousand fears. Like a lovely tree, which is one of the most beautiful things on earth, fear, which is so ugly, has also got many branches, many leaves, many expressions. Do you want to deal with the expressions, the surface, the outside? Or do we go together into the root of it? So let's together find out what is the cause of fear. We know all the expressions of fear. So if we can find the root of it, the expressions can wither away.

So what is the cause, or causation, of fear? If this question is put to you, would you answer it? Or do you expect someone else to explain it? The explanation is not the fact. You may paint a marvelous picture of a mountain, but that picture is not the mountain. The word *fear* is not fear. But the word *fear* may evoke fear. So we are not dealing with the description, with the word, but with the depth and the strength of fear. And we are trying to find out together—not I explain and you accept—the truth for ourselves, so that it is your truth and not somebody else's truth. You can't live with someone else's truth, you can only live with truth.

What is the cause of it? Is it thought? Is it time? Let's look at it. I am living, one is living, now. And thought says, "I might die tomorrow" or "I might lose my job," "I have my money in the bank, but the bank may fail," "I am all right with my wife, but she may turn to somebody else tomorrow," "I have published a book, and I hope it will be a great success," which means fear. "I want to be well known"—which is the most childish thing in the world—"I want to be well known, and somebody else is already much better known than I am." So there is this thinking that I might lose, I might gain, I might be lonely. So thinking is one of the factors of fear. I am all right with my friends, my wife, and my children, but I have also experienced the sense of desperate loneliness. Don't you know it? A sense of deep, frightening loneliness. And I am frightened. Have you ever examined what loneliness is? Why it happens? Don't you have this feeling of loneliness? Am I saying something abnormal? You must all be saints!

What then is this loneliness that causes attachment, holding on to something however illusory, however false, however meaningless? I hold on to my wife. I hold on to my club, to my God, to my ritual, to my friends, because if I let go, I am utterly lonely. Have you ever gone into that question: why human beings are so frightened of loneliness? They may live with a group, they may follow some guru and all the rest of that nonsense, but strip them of all their decoration and they are what they are, lonely. Why? What is loneliness? Not to have any relationship with anything, with nature, with another, with a friend or woman or the man with whom I have lived, all that somehow has withdrawn, I am left utterly empty, lonely—why? What is this feeling of utter despair? I will explain, but the explanation is not the fact, the word is not the thing. This needs to be very clear. Your name, Mr. Smith, is not you, the word is not you.

So explanation is not the reality, the truth. So look at it, let's look at it without the word, without the word *loneliness*. Can you do it? To look at that feeling without using the word *lonely* or *despair*. Loneliness comes when all our days are spent in self-centeredness. The very activity of self-centeredness is producing loneliness, because it is narrowing my whole life, the vast extraordinary existence of life, into a little "me." When one realizes there is that feeling, "My God, how lonely I am," to face it, to be with it completely, not move away from it, then there is a radical change.

So we must come back to this question of fear. We said thought is one of the causes of fear, obviously. I am thinking about death because I am an old man or young and see a hearse going by with all the flowers, horses, cars. And I see thought is one of the causes of fear. It is an obvious fact. And also time is a factor of fear. I am afraid of what might happen. I am afraid of something I have done which others may use as blackmail. So time and thought are the root of·fear. Time and thought. There is no division between thought and time, thought is time.

Thought is necessary, time is necessary. To go from here to there, time is necessary, and thought is necessary to drive a car, to take a bus or train. Thought is necessary, time is necessary at that level. Now I am saying, as thought and time are the root of fear, are thought and time necessary psychologically? Are they? As long you think time and thought are necessary in the psychological world, the world of the self, of the psyche, the world inside the skin, then you will be perpetually in fear.

If you perceive that—if there is perception, not acceptance—that thought and time are the root of fear, then thought and time are necessary at the physical level but inwardly are not. Therefore, the brain is actively watching itself every minute to see that thought and time do not enter the realm where they are not necessary. This requires great attention, awareness, so that the brain, which has accumulated fear for centuries, or for a day, sees where they are necessary and where they are not. It watches like a hawk so that thought and time don't enter into the whole process of living. This is real discipline, this is learning. The root meaning of that word is disciple, one who learns, who is learning all the time, who never says "I have learned" and halts.

In Observation One Begins to Discover the Lack of Freedom

O NE OF OUR GREAT problems must be to know what is freedom, and the need to understand this problem must be fairly immense and continuous since there is so much propaganda, from so many specialists; there are so many and various forms of outward and inward compulsion, and all the chaotic, contradictory persuasions, influences, and impressions. I am sure we must have asked ourselves the question: what is freedom? And as you and I know, everywhere in the world authoritarianism is spreading—not only at the political, social, and economic levels, but also at the so-called spiritual level.

Everywhere there is a compelling environmental influence. Newspapers tell us what to think, and there are so many five-, ten-, or fifteen-year plans. Then there are these specialists at the economic, scientific, and bureaucratic levels: there are all the traditions of everyday activity, what we must do and not do; the whole influence of the so-called sacred books; and there is the cinema, the radio, the newspaper: everything in the world is trying to tell us what to do, what to think and what not to think. I do not know if you have noticed how increasingly difficult it has become to think for oneself! We have become such experts in quoting what other people say, or have said, and in the midst of this authoritarian welter, where is the freedom? And what do we mean by freedom? Is there such a thing? I am using that word *freedom* in its simplest sense in which is included liberation, the mind that is liberated, free. I want, if I may, to go into that.

First, I think we must realize that our minds are really not free. Everything we see, every thought we have, shapes our mind; whatever you think now, whatever you have thought in the past, and whatever you are going to think in the future, it all shapes the mind. You think what you have been told either by the religious person or the politician, by the teacher in your school, or by books and newspapers. Everything about you influences what you think. What you eat, what you look at, what you listen to, your wife, your husband, your child, your neighbor, everything is shaping the mind. I think that is fairly obvious. Even when you think that there is a God or that there is no God, that also is the influence of tradition. So our mind is a field in which there are many contradictory influences which battle one against the other.

Do please listen, because, as I have been saying, unless we directly experience all this for ourselves, a talk of this kind has no value at all. Unless you experience what is being said, not merely follow the description but are aware, are cognizant, know the ways of your own thinking, and thereby experience, this will have no meaning whatsoever. After all, I am only describing what is actually taking place in one's life, in one's environment, so that we can be aware of it, and see if we can break through it, and what the implications of breaking through are. Because obviously we are now slaves, either a Hindu slave, a Catholic slave, a Russian slave, or a slave of one kind or another. We are all slaves to certain forms of thought, and in the midst of all that we ask if we can be free and talk about the anatomy of freedom and authority!

I think it must be fairly obvious to most of us that what we think is conditioned. Whatever your thought—however noble and wide, or however limited and petty—it is conditioned, and if you further that thought, there can be no freedom of thought. Thought itself is conditioned, because thought is the reaction of memory, and memory is the residue of all your experiences, which in turn are the result of your conditioning. So if one realizes that all thinking, at whatever level, is conditioned, then we will see that thinking is not the means of breaking through this limitation—which does not mean that we must go into some blank or speculative silence.

The actual fact is, isn't it, that every thought, every feeling, every action is conformative, conditioned, influenced. For instance, a saint comes along and by his rhetoric, gestures, looks, by quoting this and that, he influences you. And we want to be influenced. We are afraid to move away from every form of influence and see if we can go deeply and discover if there is a state of being which is not the result of influence.

Why are we influenced? In politics, as you know, it is the job of the politician to influence us; and every book, every teacher, every guru—the more powerful, the more eloquent the better we like it—imposes his thought, his way of life, his manner of conduct, upon us. So life is a battle of ideas, a battle of influences, and your mind is the field of that battle. The politician wants your mind; the guru wants your mind; the saint says, do this and not that, and he also wants your mind; and every tradition, every form of habit or custom, influences, shapes, guides, controls your mind. I think that is fairly obvious. It would be absurd to deny it. The fact is there.

You know, if I may digress a little, I think it is essential to appreciate beauty. The beauty of the sky, of the sun upon a hill, the beauty of a smile, face, gesture, the beauty of moonlight on water, of fading clouds, the song of a bird, it is essential to look at it, to feel it, to be with it. I think this is the very first requirement for a man who would seek truth. Most of us are so unconcerned with this extraordinary universe about us: we never even see the waving of a leaf in the wind; we never watch a blade of grass, touch it with our hand and know the quality of its being. This is not just being poetic, so please do not go off into a fanciful, emotional state. I say it is essential to have that deep feeling for life and not be caught in intellectual ramifications, discussions, passing examinations, quoting and brushing something new aside by saying it has already been said. Intellect is not the way. Intellect will not solve our problems; the intellect will not give us that nourishment which is imperishable. The intellect can reason, discuss, analyze, come to a conclusion from inferences and so on, but intellect is limited because it is the result of our conditioning. But sensitivity is not. Sensitivity has no conditioning; it takes you right out of the field of fears and anxieties. The mind that is not sensitive to everything about it—to the mountain, the telegraph pole, the lamp, the voice, the smile, everything—is incapable of finding what is true.

But we spend our days and years in cultivating the intellect, in arguing, discussing, fighting, struggling to be something, and so on. And yet this extraordinarily wonderful world, this earth that is so rich—not the Bombay earth, the Punjab earth, the Russian earth, or the American earth—this earth is ours, yours and mine, and that is not sentimental nonsense, it is a fact. But unfortunately we have divided it up through our pettiness, through our provincialism. And we know why we have done it—for our security, for better jobs and more jobs. That is the political game that is being played throughout the world, and so we forget to be human beings, to live happily on this earth which is ours, and to make something of it. And it is because we do not have that feeling for beauty which is not sentimental, not corrupting, not sexual, but a sense of caring, it is because we have lost that feeling—or perhaps we have never had it—that we are fighting, battling with each other over words, and have no immediate understanding of anything.

Look what you are doing in India, breaking up the land into sections, fighting and butchering, and this is happening all over the world, and for what? To have better jobs, more jobs, more power? And so in this battle we lose that quality of mind which can see things freely, happily, and without envy. We do not know how to see somebody who is happy, driving a luxurious car, and to look at him and be happy with him. Nor do we know how to sympathize with the very, very poor. We are envious of the man with the car, and we avoid the man who has nothing.

So there is no love, and without that quality of love, which is really the very essence of beauty, do what you will—go on all the pilgrimages in the world, go to every temple, cultivate all the virtues you can think of—you will get nowhere at all. Please believe me, you will not have it, that sense of beauty and love, even if you sit cross-legged for meditation, holding your breath for the

next ten thousand years. You laugh, but you do not see the trag-
edy of it. We are not in that sensitive state of mind which receives, which sees immediately something that is true. You know,
a sensitive mind is a defenseless mind, it is a vulnerable mind, and
the mind must be vulnerable for truth to enter—the truth that
you have no sympathy, the truth that you are envious.

It is essential then to have this sense of beauty, for the feeling
of beauty is the feeling of love. As I said, this is a slight digression,
but I think it is significant in relation to what we are talking about.
We are saying that a mind that is influenced, shaped, authority-
bound, can obviously never be free; and whatever it thinks, however lofty its ideals, however subtle and deep, it is still conditioned. I think it is very important to understand that the mind,
through time, through experience, through the many thousands
of yesterdays, is shaped and conditioned and that thought is not
the way out. Which does not mean that you must be thoughtless:
on the contrary. When you are capable of understanding very
profoundly, very deeply, extensively, widely, subtly, then only
will you fully recognize how petty thinking is, how small thought
is. Then there is a breaking down of the wall of that conditioning.
Can we not see that fact—that all thought is conditioned?
Whether it is the thought of the communist, capitalist, Hindu,
Buddhist, or the person who is speaking, thinking is conditioned.
And obviously the mind is the result of time, the result of the
reactions of a thousand years and of yesterday, of a second ago
and ten years ago; the mind is the result of the period in which
you have learned and suffered and of all the influences of the past
and present. Now such a mind, obviously, cannot be free, and yet
that is what we are seeking, isn't it? You know, even in Russia, in
all the totalitarian countries where everything is controlled, there
is this search for freedom. That search is there in the beginning
for all of us when we are young, for then we are revolutionary,
we are discontented, we want to know, we are curious, we are
struggling; but soon that discontent is diverted into various channels, and there it slowly dies.

So there is always within us the demand, the urge to be free,
and we never understand it, we never go into it, we have never
searched out that deep instinctual demand. Being discontented

when young, being dissatisfied with things as they are, with the stupidities of traditional values, we gradually, as we grow older, fall into the old patterns that society has established, and we get lost. It is very difficult to keep the pure discontent, the discontent which says this is not enough; there must be something else. We all know that feeling, the feeling of otherness, which we soon translate as God, or Nirvana, and then read a book about and get lost. But this feeling of otherness, the search, the inquiry for it— that, I think, is the beginning of the real urge to be free from all these political, religious, and traditional influences, and to break through that wall. Let us inquire into it.

There are, surely, several kinds of freedom. There is political freedom; there is the freedom which knowledge gives, when you know how to do things, know-how; the freedom of a wealthy man who can go round the world; the freedom of capacity, to be able to write, to express oneself, to think clearly. Then there is freedom from something; freedom from oppression, envy, tradition, ambition, and so on. And then there is the freedom which is gained, we hope, at the end—at the end of discipline, at the end of acquiring virtue, at the end of effort, the ultimate freedom we hope to get through doing certain things. So the freedom that capacity gives, the freedom from something, and the freedom we are supposed to gain at the end of a virtuous life—those are types of freedom we all know. Now are not those various freedoms merely reactions? When you say, "I want to be free from anger," that is merely a reaction: it is not freedom from anger. And the freedom which you think that you will get at the end of a virtuous life, by struggle, by discipline, that is also a reaction to what has been.

Please, follow this carefully, because I am going to say something somewhat difficult in the sense that you will not be accustomed to it. There is a sense of freedom that is not from anything, which has no cause, but which is a state of being free. You see, the freedom that we know is always brought about by will, isn't it? I will be free: I will learn a technique; I will become a specialist; I will study. And that will give me freedom. So we use will as a means of achieving freedom. I do not want to be poor, and therefore, I exercise my capacity, my will, everything to get rich. Or,

I am vain and I exercise will not to be vain. So we think we shall get freedom through the exercise of will. But will does not bring freedom; on the contrary, as I will show you.

What is will? I will be, I must not be, I am going to struggle to become something, I am going to learn—all these are forms of exercising will. Now what is this will, and how is it formed? Obviously through desire. Our many desires, with their frustrations, compulsions, and fulfillments, form as it were the threads of a cord, a rope. That is will, isn't it? Your many contradictory desires together become a very strong and powerful rope with which you try to climb to success, to freedom. Now will desire give freedom, or is the very desire for freedom the denial of it? Please watch yourselves, your own desires, your own ambition, your own will. And if one has no will and is merely being driven, that also is a part of will—the will not to resist and to go with the tide. Through that weight of desire, through that rope, we hope to climb to God, to bliss or whatever it is.

So I am asking you whether your will is a liberating factor. Does freedom come about through will? Or is freedom something entirely different, which has nothing to do with reaction, which cannot be achieved through capacity, through thought, experience, discipline, or constant conformity? That is what all the books say. Conform to the pattern and you will be free in the end; do all these things, obey, and ultimately there will be freedom. To me that is all sheer nonsense, because freedom is at the beginning, not at the end, as I will show you. To see something true is possible, isn't it? You can see that the sky is blue—and thousands of people have said so—but you can see that it is so for yourself. You can see for yourself, if you are at all sensitive, the movement of a leaf. From the very beginning there is the capacity to perceive that which is true, instinctively, not through any form of compulsion, adjustment, conformity. Now, I will show you another truth.

I say that a leader, a follower, a virtuous man does not know love. I say that to you. You who are leaders, who are followers, who are struggling to be virtuous, I say that you do not know love. Do not argue with me for a moment; do not say, "Prove it." I will reason with you, show you, but first, please listen to what I have to say, without being defensive, aggressive, approving or denying. I say that a leader, a follower, or a man who is trying to be virtuous, such an individual does not know what love is. If you really listen to that statement, not with an aggressive nor a submissive mind, then you will see the actual truth of it. If you do not see the truth of it, it is because you do not want to, or are so supremely contented with your leadership, your following, or your so-called virtues that you deny everything else. But if you are at all sensitive, inquiring, open as when looking out of a window, then you must see the truth of it, you are bound to.

Now I will give you the reasons, because you are all fairly reasonable, intellectual people and you can be convinced. But you will never actually know the truth through intellect or reason. You will be convinced through reason, but being convinced is not the perception of what is true. There is a vast difference between the two. A man who is convinced of something is incapable of seeing what is true. A man who is convinced can be unconvinced and convinced again in a different way. But a man who sees that which is true is not "convinced"; he sees that it just is true.

Now a leader who says, I know the way, I know all about life, I have experienced ultimate reality—I have the goods!—is obviously very concerned about himself and his visions and about transmitting his visions to the poor listener. A leader wants to lead people to something which he thinks is right. So a leader, whether he is a political, social, or religious leader, or whether it is your wife or husband, such a one has no love. He may talk about love, he may offer to show you the way of love, he may do all the things that love is supposed to do, but the actual feeling of love is not there—because he is a leader. If there is love, you cease to be a leader, for love exercises no authority. And the same applies to the follower. The moment you follow, you are accepting authority—the authority which gives you security, a safe corner in heaven or a safe corner in this world. When you follow, seeking security for yourself, your family, your race, your nation, that following indicates that you want to be safe, and a man who seeks safety knows no quality of love. And so also with the virtuous man. The man who cultivates humility surely is not virtuous. Humility is not a thing to be cultivated.

I am trying to show you that a mind that is sensitive, inquiring, a mind that is really listening can perceive the truth of something immediately. But truth cannot be "applied." If you see the truth, it operates without your conscious effort, of its own accord.

So discontent is the beginning of freedom, and as long as you are trying to manipulate discontent, to accept authority in order that this discontent shall disappear, enter into safe channels, then you are already losing that pristine sense of real feeling. Most of us are discontented, either with our jobs, our relationships, or whatever we are doing. You want something to happen, to change, to move, to break through. You do not know what it is. There is a constant searching, inquiring, especially when one is young, open, sensitive. Later on, as you become old, you settle down in your habits, your job, because your family is safe, your wife will not run away. So this extraordinary flame disappears and you become respectable, petty, and thoughtless.

As I have said, freedom from something is not freedom. You are trying to be free from anger; I do not say you must not be free from anger, but I say that that is not freedom. I may be rid of greed, pettiness, envy, or a dozen other things, and yet not be free. Freedom is a quality of the mind. That quality does not come about through very careful, respectable searching and inquiry, through very careful analysis or putting ideas together. That is why it is important to see the truth that the freedom we are constantly demanding is always from something, such as freedom from sorrow. Not that there is no freedom from sorrow, but the demand to be free from it is merely a reaction and therefore does not free you from sorrow. Am I making myself clear?

I am in sorrow for various reasons, and I say I must be free. The urge to be free of sorrow is born out of pain. I suffer, because of my husband, or my son, or something else, I do not like the state I am in, and I want to get away from it. That desire for freedom is a reaction, it is not freedom. It is just another desirable state I want in opposition to what is. The man who can travel around the world because he has plenty of money is not necessarily free; nor is the man who is clever or efficient, for his wanting to be free is again merely a reaction. So can I see that freedom, liberation, cannot be learned or acquired or sought after through any reaction? Therefore, I must understand the reaction; and I must also understand that freedom does not come through any effort of will. Will and freedom are contradictory, as thought and freedom are contradictory. Thought cannot produce freedom because thought is conditioned. Economically you can, perhaps, arrange the world so that man can be more comfortable, have more food, clothing, and shelter, and you may think that is freedom. Those are necessary and essential things, but that is not the totality of freedom. Freedom is a state and quality of mind. And it is that quality we are inquiring into. Without that quality, do what you will, cultivate all the virtues in the world, you will not have that freedom.

So how is that sense of otherness, that quality of mind to come about? You cannot cultivate it because the moment you use your brain, you are using thought, which is limited. Whether it is the thought of the Buddha or anyone else, all thought is limited. So our inquiry must be negative; we must come to that freedom obliquely, not directly. Am I giving some indication, or none at all? That freedom is not to be sought after aggressively, is not to be cultivated by denials, disciplines, by checking yourself, torturing yourself, by doing various exercises and all the rest of it. Like virtue, it must come without your knowing. Cultivated virtue is not virtue; the virtue which is true virtue is not self-conscious. Surely a man who has cultivated humility, who, because of his conceit, vanity, arrogance has made himself humble, such a man has no true sense of humility. Humility is a state in which the mind is not conscious of its own quality, as a flower which has fragrance is not conscious of its own perfume. So this freedom cannot be got through any form of discipline, nor can a mind which is undisciplined understand it. You use discipline to produce a result, but freedom is not a result. If it is a result, it is no longer free because it has been produced.

So how is the mind, which is full of multitudinous influences, compulsions, various forms of contradictory desires, the product of time, how is that mind to have the quality of freedom? We know that all the things that I have been talking about are not freedom. They are all manufactured by the mind under various stresses, compulsions, and influences. So, if I can approach it negatively, in the very awareness that all this is not freedom, then the mind is already disciplined—but not disciplined to achieve a result. Let us go into that briefly. The mind says, I must discipline myself in order to achieve a result. That is fairly obvious. But such discipline does not bring freedom. It brings a result because you have a motive, a cause which produces the result, but that result is never freedom, it is only a reaction. That is fairly clear. Now, if I begin to understand the way that kind of discipline operates, then, in the very process of understanding, inquiring, going into it, my mind is truly disciplined. I do not know if you can see what I mean—quickly. The exercise of will to produce a result is called discipline; whereas the understanding of the whole significance of will, of that kind of discipline, and of what we call result, demands a mind that is extraordinarily clear and "disciplined"—not by the will but through negative understanding.

So, negatively, I have understood the whole problem of what freedom is not. I have examined it, I have searched my heart and my mind, the recesses of my being, to understand what freedom means, and I see that none of these things we have described is freedom, because they are all based on desire, compulsion, will, on what I will get at the end, and they are all reactions. I see factually that they are not freedom. Therefore, because I have understood those things, my mind is open to find out or receive that which is free.

Then my mind has a quality which is not that of a disciplined mind seeking a result, nor that of an undisciplined mind that wanders about; but it has understood, negatively, both the "what is" and the "what should be," and so can perceive, can understand that freedom which is not from something, that freedom which is not a result.

This requires a great deal of inquiry. If you just repeat that there is a freedom which is not the freedom from something, it has no meaning. So please do not say it! Or if you say "I want to get that other freedom," you are also on the wrong track, for you cannot. The universe cannot enter into the petty mind; the immeasurable cannot come to a mind that knows measurement. So our whole inquiry is how to break through the measurement—which does not mean I must go off to an ashram, become neurotic, devotional, and all that nonsense.

And here, if I may say so, what is important is the teaching and not the teacher. The person who speaks here at the moment is not important—throw him overboard! What is important is what is being said. So the mind only knows the measurable, the compass of itself, the frontiers, ambitions, hopes, desperation, misery, sorrows, and joys. Such a mind cannot invite freedom. All that it can do is to be aware of itself and not condemn what it sees; not condemn the ugly or cling to the beautiful, but see what is. The mere perception of what is, is the beginning of the breaking down of the measurement of the mind, of its frontiers, its patterns. Just to see things as they are. Then you will find that the mind can come to that freedom involuntarily, without knowing. This transformation in the mind itself is the true revolution. All other revolutions are reactions, even though they use the word *freedom* and promise Utopia, the heavens, everything. There is only true revolution in the quality of the mind.

A Radical Mutation in the Mind

———

QUESTIONER: Could we speak about the brain and the mind? Thinking takes place materially in the brain cells. That is, thinking is a material process. If thinking stops and there is perception without thought, what happens to the material brain? You seem to say that mind has its place outside the brain, but where does the movement of pure perception take place if not somewhere in the brain? And how is it possible for mutation to take place in the brain cells if pure perception has no connection in the brain?

KRISHNAMURTI: Have you got the question? First, the questioner says he wants to differentiate between the brain and the mind. Then he asks if perception is purely outside the brain, which means thought is not the movement of perception. And he asks, if perception takes place outside the brain, which is the thinking and remembering process, what happens to the brain cells themselves, which are conditioned by the past? And will there be a mutation in the brain cells if perception is outside? Is this clear?

So let's begin with the brain and the mind. The brain is a material function. It is a muscle—right? Like the heart. And the brain cells contain all the memories. Please, I am not a brain specialist, nor have I studied the experts, but I have lived a long time now and I have watched a great deal, not only the reaction of others—what they say, what they think, what they want to tell me—but also I have watched how the brain reacts. So the brain has evolved through time from the single cell, taking millions of years, until it reached the ape and went on another million years until man could stand, and so ultimately there is the human brain. The human brain is contained within the skull, but it can go beyond itself. You can sit here and think of your country, or your home—and in thought, not physically, you are instantly there.

The brain has extraordinary capacity, and technologically it has done the most extraordinary things. But the brain has also been conditioned by the limitation of language, not by language itself but by the limitation of language. It has been conditioned by the climate it lives in, by the food one eats, by the social environment, the society in which it lives, and that society has been created by the brain. So that society is not different from the activities of the brain. It has been conditioned by millions of years of accumulated knowledge based on experience, which is tradition. I am British, you are German, he is a Hindu, he is a black man, he is this, he is that, there is all the nationalistic division, which is tribal division—and the religious conditioning. So the brain is conditioned, and being conditioned it is limited. The brain has extraordinary capacity, unlimited in the technological world, with computers and so on, but it is very, very limited with regard to the psyche.

Although people have said "Know yourself" from the Greeks, from the ancient Hindus, and so on, they never study their own psyche. The psychologists, the philosophers, the experts, study the psyche of another but they never study their own. They study rats, rabbits, pigeons, monkeys, and so on, but never say, "I am going to look at myself. I am ambitious, I am greedy, I am envious, I compete with my neighbor, my fellow scientists." It is the same psyche that has existed for thousands of years, and though outwardly we are technologically marvelous, inwardly we are very primitive.

So the brain is limited, primitive, in the world of the psyche. Now can that limitation be broken down? Can that limitation, which is the self, the ego, the "me," self-centered concern, can all that be wiped away? Which means the brain is then unconditioned—you understand what I am saying? Then it has no fear.

Now most of us live in fear, are anxious, frightened of what is going to happen, frightened of death, of a dozen things. Can all that be wiped away completely and be fresh? So that the brain is free and its relationship to the mind is then entirely different. That is, to see that one has no shadow of the self. And that is extraordinarily arduous, to see the "me" doesn't enter into any field. The self hides in many ways, under every stone. The self can hide in compassion, going to India and looking after poor people, because the self then is attached to some idea, faith, conclusion, belief. The self has many masks, the mask of meditation, the mask of achieving the highest, the mask that I am enlightened, that I know of what I speak. All this concern about humanity is another mask. So one has to have an extraordinary, subtle, quick brain to see where it is hiding. It requires great attention, watching, watching, watching. You won't do all this. Probably you are all too lazy, or too old and say "For God's sake, all this isn't worth it, leave me alone." But if one really wants to go into this very deeply, one has to watch like a hawk every movement of thought, every movement of reaction, so the brain can be free from its conditioning. The speaker is speaking for himself, not for anybody else. He may be deceiving himself, he may be trying to pretend to be something or other. He may be, you don't know. So have a great deal of skepticism, doubt, question, not accepting what others say.

So when there is no conditioning of the brain, it no longer degenerates. As you get older—perhaps not you—but generally as people get older, their brain begins to wear out, they lose their memory, they behave in a peculiar way, you know all that. Degeneration is not merely in America, degeneration takes place in the brain first. And when the brain is completely free of the self and therefore no longer conditioned, then we can ask: what is the mind? The ancient Hindus inquired into the mind, and they posited various statements about it. But wiping all that out, not depending on somebody, however ancient, however traditional, what is the mind? Our brain is constantly in conflict and therefore in disorder. Such a brain cannot understand what the mind is. The mind—not my mind, the mind, the mind that has created the universe, the mind that has created the cell, that mind which is pure energy and intelligence—can have a relationship to the brain only when the brain is free. But if the brain is conditioned, there is no relationship. You don't have to believe all this! So intelligence is the essence of that mind, not the intelligence of thought, not the intelligence of disorder. But it is pure order, pure intelligence, and therefore, it is pure compassion. And that mind has a relationship with the brain when the brain is free.

I could go into this a lot more, but I won't. Are you getting tired, or are you listening? Are you listening to yourself, or are you just listening to me? Are you doing both? Are you watching your own reactions, how your brain works? That is, action, reaction, back and forth, back and forth, which means you are not listening. You are only listening when this action, reaction stops, so there is just pure listening. Look, the sea is in constant movement. The tide is coming in, the tide is going out. This is its action. And human beings are also like this—there is action and reaction, that reaction produces another reaction, that reaction in me produces another one, and so back and forth. When there is that movement back and forth, there is naturally no quietness. And it is only in that quietness that you can hear the truth or the falseness, not when you are back and forth, back and forth. At least see it intellectually, logically, that if there is constant movement, you are not listening, how can you? You can listen only when there is absolute silence. See the logic of it. And is it possible to stop this movement back and forth?

The speaker says it is possible when you have studied yourself, when you have gone into yourself very deeply, when you understand yourself, then you can say the movement has really stopped.

And the questioner asks: as the mind is outside, not contained in the brain, how can perception, which takes place only when there is no activity of thought, bring about a mutation in the brain cells, which are a material process?

Look, keep it very simple. This is one of our difficulties. We never look at a complex thing very simply. This is a very complex question, but we must begin very simply to understand something very vast. So let's begin simply. Traditionally you have pursued a certain path, religiously, economically, socially, morally, and so on, in a certain direction all your life. Suppose I have done this. You come along and say, "Look, the way you are going leads nowhere; it will bring you much more trouble, you will keep killing each other everlastingly, you will have tremendous economic difficulty." And you give me logical reasons, examples, and so on. But I say, "No, sorry, this is my way of doing things." And I keep on going that way; most people do, ninety-nine percent of people keep going that way, including the gurus, the philosophers, the newly "enlightened" people. And you come along and say, "Look, that is a dangerous path, don't go there. Turn and go in another direction entirely." And you convince me, you show me the logic, the reason, the sanity of it, and I turn and go in a totally different direction.

What has taken place? I have been going in one direction all my life; you come along and say, "Don't go there, it is dangerous, it leads nowhere. You will have more troubles, more aches, more problems. Go in another direction, things will be entirely different." And I accept your logic, your statements, sanely, and I move in another direction. What has happened to the brain? Keep it simple. Going in that direction, suddenly move in the other direction, the brain cells have themselves changed. You understand? I have broken the tradition. It is as simple as that. But the tradition is so strong, it has all its roots in my present existence, and you are asking me to do something which I rebel against; therefore, I do not listen. Or instead I listen to find out if what you are saying is true or false. I want to know the truth of the matter, not what I wish for or what pleases me, but to know the truth of it; therefore, being serious I listen with all my being and I see you are quite right. I have moved. In that movement there is a change in the brain cells. It is as simple as that.

Suppose I am a practicing Catholic, or a devout Hindu, and you come and tell me, "Look, don't be silly, all that is nonsense. It is just tradition, words without much meaning, though the words have accumulated meaning." You point this out and I see what you say is the truth; I move, I am free from that conditioning; therefore, there is a change, a mutation in the brain. Or I have been brought up, we have all been brought up, to live with fear. And you tell me it can end, and instinctively I say, "Show it, let's go together, find out." I want to find out if what you are saying is true or false, whether fear can really end. So I spend time, I discuss with you, I want to find out, learn, so my brain is active to find out, not to be told what to do. So the moment I begin to inquire, work, look, watch the whole movement of fear, then either I accept it and say, "Well, I like to live in fear," or I move away from it. When you see that, there is a change in the brain cells.

It is so simple if you could only look at this thing very simply. There is a mutation—to make it a little more complex—in the very brain cells, not through any effort, not through the will or through any motive, when there is perception. Perception is when there is observation without a movement of thought. When there is the absolute silence of memory, which is time, which is thought—to look at something without the past. Do it. Look at the speaker without all the remembrance that you have accumulated about him. Watch him, or watch your father, your mother, your husband, wife, girl, and so on—it doesn't matter what—watch without any past remembrance and hurt and guilt and all that coming into being. Just watch. When you so watch without any prejudice, then there is freedom from that which has been.

Total Negation Is the Essence
of the Positive

———

To FIND OUT WHAT is true and not follow another who tells you what is true, or arbitrarily asserts what is false and what is true, you must see that which is intrinsically false and put it away. In other words, one finds out what is true, surely, only through negation. Say, for instance, you realize that you cannot have a quiet mind as long as there is greed. So you address yourself not to quietness of the mind, but to greed. You investigate to see if greed, or avarice, or envy can be put away completely. There is a constant purgation of the mind, a constant process of negation.

If I want to understand the whole of this extraordinary thing called life, which must include the totality of all religions; if I want to be sensitive to it, appreciate it, and I see that nationalism, provincialism, or any limited attitude is most destructive to that understanding, what happens? Surely, I realize that I must put away nationalism, that I must cease to be a Hindu or a Muslim or a Christian. I must cease to have this insular, nationalistic attitude, and be free of the authority of organized religion, dogma, and belief. So through negation, the mind begins to perceive what is true. But most of us find it very difficult to understand through negation, because we think it will lead nowhere, give us nothing.

We say it will create a state of vacuum—as though our minds were not in a state of vacuum now!

To understand the immensity, the timeless quality of life, surely you must approach it through negation. It is because you are committed to a particular course of action, a certain pattern of existence, that you find it difficult to free yourself from all that and face a new way, a new approach. After all, death is the ultimate negation. It is only when one dies now, while living, which means the constant breaking of all habit-patterns, the various attitudes, conclusions, ideas, beliefs that one has—it is only then that one can find out what life is. But most of us say, "I cannot break the pattern, it is impossible, so I must learn a way of breaking it; I must practice a certain system, a method of breaking it." So we become slaves to the new pattern which we establish through practice. We have not broken the pattern, but have only substituted a new pattern for the old.

You nod your heads, you say this is so true, logical, clear—and you go right on with the pattern, whether old or new! It seems to me that the real problem is the sluggishness of the mind. Any fairly intelligent mind can see that inwardly we want security, a haven, a refuge where we shall not be disturbed, and that this urge to be secure creates a pattern of living which becomes a habit. But to break that pattern requires a great deal of energy, thought, inquiry, and the mind refuses, because it says, "If I break my pattern of life, what will become of me? What will this school be if the old pattern is broken? It will be chaos"—as if it were not chaos now!

You see, we are always living in a state of contradiction from which we act, and therefore, we create still more contradiction, more misery. We have made living a process of action versus being. The man who is very clever, who convinces others through his gift of gab or his way of life, who puts on a loincloth and outwardly becomes a saint, may inwardly be acting from a state of contradiction. He may be a disastrously torn entity, but because he has the outward paraphernalia of a saintly life, we all follow him blindly. Whereas if we really go into and understand this problem of contradiction within and without, then I think we shall come upon an action which is not away from life, but which is part of our daily existence. Such action does not spring from idea, but from being. It is the comprehension of the whole of life.

I wonder if you are ever in the position of asking yourself, "What am I going to do?" If you do put that question to yourself, do you not always respond according to a pattern of thought which you have already established? You never allow yourself to ask, "What shall I do?"—and stop there. You always say, "This must be done, that must not be done." It is only the intelligent mind, the awakened mind, the mind which sees the significance of this whole process, that asks, "What shall I do, what course of action shall I take?" without a ready-made answer. Having through negation come to that point, such a mind begins to comprehend, to be sensitive to the whole problem of existence.

The Division between the Thinker and the Thought, the Observer and the Observed

---

D O PLEASE FOLLOW THIS a little. It may appear to be complex, but it isn't if you listen quietly. There is the observer and the thing observed, and there is a division between these two, and this division, this screen in between, is the word, the image, the memory, the space in which all conflict takes place, that space being the ego, the "me" which is the accumulation of words, of images, of memories from a thousand yesterdays. So consequently there is no direct contact with "what is." You either condemn "what is," rationalize it, accept it, or justify it, and as this is all verbalization, there is no direct contact, therefore no understanding, and consequently no resolution of "what is."

Look, there is envy, envy being measured comparison, and one is conditioned to accept it. Someone is bright, intelligent, successful, and the other is not. Ever since childhood one has been brought up to measure and compare. So envy is born, but one observes that envy "objectively" as something outside of oneself, whereas the observer himself is that envy. There is no actual division between the observer and the observed.

So the observer realizes that he cannot possibly do anything about that envy. He sees very clearly that whatever he does with regard to envy is still envy, because he is both the cause and the effect. Therefore, the "what is," which is our daily life with all its problems of envy, jealousy, fear, loneliness, and despair, is not different from the observer who says, "I am those things." The observer is envious, is jealous, is fearful, is lonely and full of despair. So the observer cannot do anything about "what is," which does not mean he accepts it, lives with it, or is content with it. This conflict comes about through the division between the observer and the observed, but when there is no longer any resistance to "what is," then a complete transformation takes place, and that transformation is meditation. So finding out for yourself the whole structure and nature of the observer, which is yourself, and also of the observed, which is again yourself, and realizing the totality, the unity of it is meditation, in which there is no conflict whatsoever—and therefore a complete dissolution and the going beyond of "what is."

—

Then what is the function of thinking or thought? You must have knowledge—scientific knowledge, knowledge that is the accumulated experience of man, the experience of using words, how to play a piano, and so on. You must have complete knowledge, you cannot do without technical knowledge.

And you also see what knowledge has done. You have accumulated knowledge as an experience of the thing that happened yesterday. You want that experience repeated, and it may not happen; therefore, there is pain. So knowledge is necessary in one direction, and knowledge breeds fear and pain in the other.

When you had that experience of sunset yesterday, it was new, fresh, full of joy, something incredible. The light, the texture, the feel of it that has been recorded, that has become knowledge, and therefore, that is already old. The old says, "I must have new experience," and the new experience is translated in terms of pleasure.

So you see what thought does, that thought must function logically, sanely, effectively, objectively in the technological world, and you also see the danger of thought. The question arises: what is the entity that holds the thought, the thought as pleasure, as pain? What is it that holds this memory as a center from which it operates? Have you observed that there is in you an observer and the thing observed? The observer is the censor, is the accumulated knowledge as a Christian, a Hindu, a Communist, and so on. The observer is the center, he is the ego, the "me." That "me," that ego, invents a superego, or atman, but it is still part of thought. So there is a duality in you as the observer and the observed, the "me" and the "you," we, the Hindus, and them, the Muslims. This division is the cause of all conflict.

The observer is the holder of all memory from which all thought arises, so thought is never new. It is never free. It can only think of or invent freedom.

How does one observe without the observer, the observer being the past, the observer being the image? You have built up an image about your wife or husband through time—forty or ten years or one month or one day—that image has been built up. The image-maker is the observer, and we are asking whether you can observe your wife, the tree, or husband, without the image, without the observer. To find that out, you must find out the machinery of image-building. What is it that creates images? If you understand that, you will never create an image and you can observe without the observer.

We are asking whether the image-maker, the machinery of this image-making, can ever come to an end. I will show you how it comes to an end. First of all, you have to inquire what is awareness, what it is to be aware, aware of the trees, of your neighbor, of the shape of the hall, aware of the color of the various saris, shirts, aware outwardly and aware inwardly, to be aware choicelessly.

You insult me, and at that moment of insult, if there is total awareness, there is no recording, I do not want to hit you back, I do not want to call you a name, I am passively aware of the insult or the flattery, and therefore, there is no image-making. Next time somebody insults you or flatters you, be totally aware.

Then you will see that the old structure of the brain becomes quiet, doesn't instantly operate. The recording does not record, because you are totally aware. Please see this when you go out next time, look at a tree, just observe it, see the beauty of it, the branches of it, the strength of the trunk, the curve of the branch, the delicate leaves, the shape of it, without the image, the image being the previous knowledge of your having seen that tree. So you look at it without the observer, look at your wife or your husband, as though you are seeing her for the first time—that is, without the image. This seeing is true relationship, not the relationship between image and image. Therefore, a mind that is capable of observing so clearly is capable of observing what truth is.

—

Look at the sky, look at that tree, look at the beauty of the light, look at the clouds with their curves, with their delicacy. If you look at them without any image, you have understood your own life. But you are looking at yourself, at your life, as an observer and your life as something to be observed; there is a division between the observer and the observed. This division is the essence of all conflict, the essence of all the struggle, pain, fear, despair. Where there is a division between human beings, division of nationalities, division of religion, social division, wherever there is a division, there must be conflict. There is Pakistan on one side and India on the other battling with each other. You are a Brahmin and another is a non-Brahmin, and there is hate, division. Now that externalized division with all its conflict is the same as the inward division, as the observer and the observed.

A mind that is in conflict cannot possibly ever understand what truth is. A mind in conflict is a tortured mind, a twisted mind. How can it be free to observe the beauty of the earth or a child or a beautiful woman or man or the beauty of extreme sensitivity and all that is involved in it?

Now we are going to find out for ourselves—not from the speaker—whether it is possible to end this division between the observer and the observed. Are you following all this? Please, this is important if you are really to move any further. You are going to go into the question of what love is, what death is, what the beauty of truth is, what meditation is, and a mind that is completely and totally still. And to understand all this, one must begin with the ending of conflict, and this conflict exists wherever there is the observer and the observed.

The next question is: what is this observer, the observer who has separated himself from the observed? We see that when we are angry, at the moment of anger, there is no observer. At the moment of experiencing anything, there is no observer. When you look at a sunset, that sunset is something immense; when you look at it, there is no observer saying, "I am seeing the sunset." A second later comes the observer. Supposing you are angry, at the moment of anger there is no observer, no experiencer, there is only a state of anger. A second later comes the observer who says, "I should not have been angry," or "I was justified in getting angry." This is the beginning of division.

How does this happen? Why, at the moment of experience, is there a total absence of the observer, and how does it happen that a second later the observer comes into being? When you look at this flower, at the moment you observe it closely, there is no observer, there is only a looking. Then you begin to name the flower. Then you say, "I wish I had it in my garden or in my house." Then you have already begun to build an image about that flower. The image and the image-maker are the observer, and the observer is the past, the "me" as the observer is the past, the "me" is the knowledge which I have accumulated, the knowledge of pain, sorrow, agony, suffering, despair, loneliness, jealousy. The observer looks at that flower with the eyes of the past. You do not know how to look without the observer, and therefore, you bring about conflict.

Now our question is: can you look not only at the flower but at your life, at your agony, at your despair, at your sorrow, without naming it, without saying to yourself, "I must go beyond it, I must suppress it"? Can you look at it without the observer? Take your particular form or particular tendency, or take what most people are—envious. You know what envy is. You are very famil-iar with that. Envy is comparison, the measurement of thought, a comparing of what you are with what you should be or what you would like to become. When you are envious of your neigh-bor—he has got a bigger car, a better house, and all the rest of it—you certainly feel envy, that is, you compare yourself with him and envy him more. Now can you look at that feeling with-out saying it is right or wrong, without naming it? Can you look at it without an image? Then you go beyond it. Instead of struggling with envy and trying to suppress it, observe your anger, your envy, without naming it.

The naming is the movement of the past memory while it justifies or condemns. If you can look at it without naming, then you will see that you go beyond it.

The moment you know the possibility of going beyond "what is," you are full of energy. The man who does not know how to go beyond "what is," because he does not know how to deal with it, is afraid, he wants to escape. Such a person loses energy. If you have a problem and you can solve it, then you have energy. A man who has a thousand problems and does not know what to do with them loses his energy. So in the same way, look at your life, in which there is what you call love.

What is love? We are not discussing theories of what love should be. We are observing what we call love. Is love pleasure? Is love jealousy? Can a man love who is ambitious? Can a man love who is competitive? And you are all competitive, you want a better job, better position, better house, an image of yourself. Can you love when you go through all this tyranny, when you dominate your husband, your wife, your children? When you are seeking power, is there a possibility of love?

In negating what is not love, there is love. You have to negate everything that is not love, which means no ambition, no competition, no aggression, no violence either in speech, act, or thought. When you negate that which is not love, then you know what love is. And love is something that is intense, that you feel strongly; love is not pleasure. Therefore, one must understand pleasure, and not attempt to love somebody.

—

Now let us examine what the observer is—if you have the energy to go on with this. What is the observer? Surely the observer is the past—the past, be it yesterday or a few seconds ago, or the past of many years, many years as a conditioned entity living in a particular culture. The observer is the past. The observer is the total sum of past experiences. The observer is knowledge. When I say, "I know you because I met you yesterday"; when I say, "I am a Hindu, Catholic, Protestant, Communist, Muslim"—it is the past, I have been conditioned in the culture in which I have been brought up. So the observer is the past. This is obvious, isn't it? The observer is within the field of time—to make it a little more complex. The observer is the past, which through the present modifies the future. And the future is still the observer. When he says, "I will be that," he has projected "that" from past knowledge, either pleasure, pain, suffering or delight, fear, and so on, and says, "I must become that." That is, the past going through the present which becomes modified into the future, which is a projection from the past. So the observer is the past. That is, you live in the past—don't you? Just think of it. You are the past and you live in the past. And that is your life. Past memories, past delights, past remembrances, the things that you enjoyed—and the failures, the lack of fulfillment, the misery, everything is in the past. And through the eyes of the observer you begin to judge the present, the thing that is living, moving. Are we going together?

So when I look at myself, I am looking with the eyes of the past, and therefore, I condemn, judge, evaluate, and say, "This is right, wrong, good, bad" according to the culture, the tradition, the knowledge, the experience which the observer has gathered. Therefore, it prevents observation of the living thing, which is the "me." And that "me" may not be me at all! I only know the "me" as the past. I don't know if you are following this. When the Muslim says he is a Muslim, he is the past, conditioned by the culture in which he has been brought up. As the Catholic or the Communist is. The whole thing is based on this. So when we talk about living, we are talking about living in the past. And therefore, there is conflict between the past and the present, because I am conditioned as a Muslim, or whatever, and I cannot meet the living present, which demands that I break down my conditioning. And my conditioning is deliberately brought about by my father, my forefathers, keeping me in the narrow line of their belief, their tradition, their mischief, their misery. This is what is happening all the time—not only is there conditioning by the past, the culture in which we have lived, but also by every incident, experience, happening. We live in the past. I see a beautiful sunset and I say, "How marvelous that is, look at the light, the shadows, the rays of the sun, the green light, the hills"—and it is stored up, and that memory acts tomorrow, saying, "I must look at that sun again, find again that beauty." And then I can't find it, so I struggle to find it—go to a museum—you follow? The whole circus begins.

Now can I look at myself with eyes that have never been touched by time? Time involves analysis, holding on to the past, this whole process of dreaming, recollection, gathering the past and holding it—all that. Can I look at myself without the eyes of time? Put that question to yourself. Don't say you can or you cannot. You don't know. And when you look at yourself without the eyes of time, what is there then to look? Don't answer me, please. Do you understand my question? I have looked at myself with the quality, the nature, and the structure of time, the past, I have looked at myself through the eyes of the past. I have no other eyes to look with. I have looked at myself as a Catholic, or something else, which is the past. So my eyes are incapable of looking at myself, at "what is," without time, which is the past. So I am asking a question, which is: can the eyes observe without the past?

Now let me put it differently: I have an image about myself, not only created by the culture in which I have lived, but I also have my own particular image of myself, apart from the culture. We have a great many images. I have an image about you, I have an image about my wife, children, political leader, my priest, and I have an image about what I should be, what I am not, as well as the image which culture has imposed on me. So I have quantities of images. Don't you have them?

(Audience responds, "Yes.")

Delighted! Now how can you look without an image? Because if you look with an image, it is a distortion—obviously. Isn't it? I look at you with the image which I have of you, which has been put together because you were angry with me yesterday, the image that you are not my friend anymore, you are ugly, you are this or that. Now that image distorts the perception when I meet you next time. So that image is the past, and all my images are the past. And I daren't get rid of any of those images because I don't know what it would be like without an image. So I cling to one or two images. So the mind depends on an image for its survival.

Now can the mind observe without any image—without the image of the tree, the cloud, the hills, the flowing waters, the image of my wife, my children, my husband, my aunt, without any image in relationship? It is the image that brings conflict in relationship. Right? I cannot get on with my wife because she has bullied me. That image has been built up day after day, and that image prevents any kind of relationship; perhaps we sleep together, that is irrelevant. And there is a fight. So can the mind look, observe without any image that has been put together by time? That means, can the mind observe without any image? Which means to observe without the observer, which is the past, the "me"? Can I look at you without the "me" as the conditioned entity?

QUESTIONER: It's impossible.

KRISHNAMURTI: Impossible? How do you know it is impossible? The moment you say it is impossible, then you have blocked yourself. And if you say it is possible, it is also blocking yourself. But if you say, let's find out, examine, go into it, then you will find the mind can observe without the eyes of time. And when it so observes, then what is there to be observed?

I started out learning about myself—I have explored all the possibilities, analysis, all that, and I see the observer is the past, and the mind lives in the past, because the brain has evolved in time, which is the past. And in the past there is "security." Right? My house, my wife, my belief, my status, my position, my fame, my blasted little self—in that there is great "safety," "security." And I am asking, can the mind observe without any of that? And if it so observes, what is there to see, except the hills, the flowers, the colors, the people—is there anything in me to be observed? Therefore, the mind is totally free. And you may say, What is the point of that being free? The point is: such a mind has no conflict. And such a mind is completely quiet and peaceful, not violent. And such a mind can create a new culture—a new culture, not a counterculture to the old, but a totally different thing altogether, where we shall have no conflict at all. That one has discovered, not as a theory, as a verbal statement, but as an actual fact within oneself—that the mind can observe totally and therefore without the eyes of the past, and therefore, the mind is something totally different.

—

How shall we proceed with this fairly obvious problem that our minds are conditioned, our minds are everlastingly chattering, never quiet? We try to impose quietness, or it happens casually, by chance. To proceed with this problem, to learn, to see, there must be the quietness of a mind that is not broken up, not torn apart, not tortured. If I want to see something very clearly, whether a tree, or a cloud, or the face of a person next to me, to see very clearly without any distortion, the mind must obviously not be chattering. The mind must be very quiet to observe, to see. And the very seeing is the doing and the learning. So what is meditation? Is it possible to consider, to observe, to comprehend, to learn, to see very clearly, without any distortion, to hear everything as it is, not interpreting or translating it according to one's prejudice? When you listen to the bird of a morning, is it possible to listen to it completely, without a word cropping up into your mind, to listen to it with total attention, to listen to it without saying how beautiful, how lovely, what a lovely morning?

All that means that the mind must be silent, and the mind cannot be silent when there is any form of distortion. That is why one must understand every form of conflict, whether between the individual and society, between the individual and the neighbor, between oneself, wife, husband, children, and so on. Any form of conflict, at any level, is a distorting process. When there is contradiction within oneself which arises when one wants to express oneself in various different ways and one cannot, then there is conflict, struggle, pain, which distorts the quality, the subtlety, the quickness of the mind.

Meditation is the understanding of the nature of life with its dual activity, its conflict. Seeing the true significance and truth of it, so that the mind, though it has been conditioned for thousands of years, living in conflict, struggle, battle, becomes clear, without distortion. The mind sees that distortion must take place when it follows an ideology, the idea of what should be as opposed to what is, hence a duality, a conflict, a contradiction, and hence a mind that is tortured, perverted.

There is only one thing. That which is, "what is," nothing else. To be completely concerned with "what is" puts away every form of duality and hence there is no conflict, no tortured mind. So meditation is a mind seeing actually "what is," without interpreting or translating it, without wishing it were not, or accepting it.

A mind can only do this when the "observer" ceases to be.

Please, this is important to understand. Most of us are afraid. So there is fear, and the one who wants to get rid of fear is the "observer." The "observer" is the entity who "recognizes" the new fear and translates it in terms of the old fears known and stored up from the past, and from which it has escaped. So as long as there is the "observer" and the thing observed, there must be duality and hence conflict, and the mind becomes twisted. And that is one of the most complicated states, something which we must understand. As long as there is the "observer," there must be the conflict of duality.

Is it possible to go beyond the "observer"—the "observer" being the whole accumulation of the past, the "me," the ego, the thought which springs from this accumulated past?

I hope, as the speaker is putting this into words, you are listening to and observing it very clearly, to see if it is possible to eliminate all conflict so that the mind can be utterly at peace—not contented; contentment arises only when there is dissatisfaction, which again is the process of duality. When there is no "observer" but only observing and hence no conflict, then only can there be complete peace. Otherwise there is violence, aggression, brutality, wars, and all the rest of the ways of modern life.

So meditation is the understanding of thought and discovering for oneself whether thought can come to an end. It is only then, when the mind is silent, that it can see actually "what is" without any distortion, hypocrisy, or self-delusion. There are the systems and gurus who say that to end thought, you must learn concentration, learn control. But a disciplined mind, in the sense of being disciplined to imitate, to conform, to accept and obey, is always frightened. Such a mind can never be still, it can only pretend to be still. And the quiet mind is not possible through the use of any drug or through the repetition of words. You can reduce it to dullness, but it is not quiet.

Meditation is the ending of sorrow, the ending of thought which breeds fear and sorrow, the fear and sorrow in daily life, when you are married, when you are in business. In business you must use your technological knowledge, but when that knowledge is used for psychological purposes to become more powerful, to occupy a position that gives you prestige, honor, fame, it breeds only antagonism and hatred. Such a mind can never understand what truth is. Meditation is the understanding of the way of life, it is the understanding of sorrow and fear and going beyond them. To go beyond them is not merely to grasp intellectually or rationally the significance of the process of sorrow and fear, but it is to go actually beyond them. And to go beyond is to observe and to see very clearly sorrow and fear as they are. In that seeing very clearly, the "observer" must come to an end.

Meditation is the way of life, it is not an escape from life. Meditation is obviously not the experiencing of visions or having strange mystical experiences. As you know, you can take a mind-expanding drug that will produce certain reactions chemically, which will make the mind highly sensitive, and in that sensitive state you may see things heightened, but it will still be according to your conditioning.

Nor is meditation the repetition of words. There has been the fashion lately of someone giving you a Sanskrit word, which you keep repeating and thereby hope to achieve some extraordinary experience—which is all utter nonsense. Of course, if you keep on repeating a lot of words, your mind is made dull and thereby quiet; but that is not meditation at all. Meditation is the constant understanding of the way of life, every minute, the mind being extraordinarily alive, alert, not burdened by any fear, any hope, any ideology, any sorrow. And if we can go together that far— and I hope some of us have been able to do so actually and not theoretically—then we enter into something quite different.

As we have already said, you cannot go very far without laying the foundation of the understanding of daily life, the daily life of loneliness, boredom, excitement, sexual pleasures, of the demands to fulfill, to express oneself, the daily life of conflict between hate and love, a life in which one demands to be loved, a life of deep inward loneliness. Without understanding all that, without distorting, without becoming neurotic, being completely, highly sensitive and balanced, without being that, you cannot go very far.

When that foundation is deeply laid, then the mind is capable of being completely quiet and therefore completely at peace— which is entirely different from being contented like a cow! Then alone is it possible to find out if there is something beyond the measure of the mind, whether there is such a thing as reality, as God, something which man has sought for millions of years; something which he has sought through his gods and temples, through sacrificing himself, by becoming a hermit and all the absurdities and inventions that man has gone through.

You know, up to now, verbal explanation, verbal communication, has to a certain point been possible. But words exist only for communicating something that may be expressed in words. It is not possible to put into words what is beyond all this. To describe it becomes utterly meaningless. All that one can do is to open the door, that door which is kept open only when there is order. Not the order of society, which is disorder, but the order that comes into being when you see actually "what is," without any distortion brought about by the "observer." When there is no distortion at all, then there is order, which in itself brings its own extraordinary, subtle discipline. And to leave that door open is all that one can do. Whether that reality comes through that door or not, one cannot invite it, and if one is very lucky, by some strange chance, it may come and give its blessing. You cannot seek it. After all, that is beauty and love, you cannot seek it. If you seek it, it becomes merely the continuation of pleasure, which is not love. There is bliss, which is not pleasure. When the mind is in that state of meditation, there is immense bliss. Then the everyday living of contradictions, brutalities, and violence has no place. But one must work very hard, every day, to lay that foundation. That is all that matters, nothing else. Then out of that silence which is the very nature of a meditative mind may come love and beauty.

—

If you can observe actually "what is" without a censor, there is a transformation of "what is." One is violent—that is apparently the normal human condition, to be violent. I am violent. At the moment of violence there is no observer, then a few seconds later the observer comes into being. He says "I should not be violent" because he has an image of nonviolence, an ideal of nonviolence—which prevents him from observing violence. So he says to himself, "Every day I will be less and less violent; day by day I will ultimately reach a state of nonviolence." Now what is implied in that simple fact that I am violent and say I will be nonviolent one day? First, there is the observer and the observed. Second, I am sowing the seeds of violence in the meantime, before I arrive at the state of nonviolence. Then there is the factor of time before I can be completely nonviolent—that is, the space between violence and nonviolence. In that, observe "what is."

How do you observe "what is"? Do you observe it with your conditioned mind, saying, "I must not be violent" with the image which you have about violence? Or is there an observation without the word, without the image? To observe without the image requires tremendous energy. You are wasting energy by suppressing violence or transforming it or pursuing an ideal of nonviolence. That is all wastage of energy.

This Division between the Observer and the Observed Is an Illusion

———

KRISHNAMURTI: I think it would be very worthwhile if we spent some time talking over together the question of awareness, attention, and meditation. We'll begin by inquiring into ourselves and finding out what we mean by awareness. Because it seems to me most of us are not aware, either of what we are talking about, or of our feelings, our environment, the colors around us, the people, the kind of cars that pass by on the road, the shape of the trees, the clouds, the movement of the water, the flight of birds—and perhaps some of you noticed this morning, very early, how extraordinarily clear and perfumed the air was. We're not really aware of these outside things at all.

Perhaps it is because we are so concerned with ourselves—our own problems, ideas, pleasures, pursuits, and ambitions—that we are not aware outwardly and objectively. And yet we talk a great deal about "being aware." Once the speaker was traveling with some people in a car. There was a chauffeur, and I was sitting beside him. Behind us three gentlemen were discussing awareness very intently and asking me questions about it. Unfortunately at that moment the driver was inattentive and ran over a goat—the three gentlemen were still discussing awareness and yet were totally unaware of what had happened! And the chauffeur was not

in the least concerned. When we pointed out this lack of awareness on the part of people who were trying to be aware, it was a
total surprise to them. And it is the same with most of us. We are
not aware either of outward or of inward things. So may we spend
some time discussing this?

Most of our minds are rather dull, insensitive, because we are
unhealthy, we've had problems we have lived with for days,
months, years on end—the problem of children, marriage, earn-
ing a livelihood, the brutal society in which we live—all that has
made us insensitive, dull, our reactions are rather slow. Such a
mind attempts to be aware, hoping thereby to somehow go beyond the limitations that society, the individual, and so on have
placed upon it. In talking about awareness, I think it is important
to understand how very simple it is—not to complicate it, not to
say "It must be this" or "It must not be that," but to begin very
simply, because it's a tremendously complex problem.

We must go into it step by step, not analytically, but observing
ourselves as we are, and being aware of what we are, and from
there move. Can we do that, just for the fun of it? I think that
will sharpen the mind, because we are rather crude, assertive, aggressive, self-important people wanting to tell others what we
think, and what they should or should not do. We want to boss
others, we assume responsibility which is none of ours. So we live
in a kind of self-important, self-projecting world of our own, and
living in that, we talk about awareness as being something extraordinarily mysterious.

If we could go into this very interesting problem very deeply,
we will take a journey without end. Shall we do that? Don't agree
with me, please. See for yourself whether it is important or not.
Because I feel that if we can understand this very simple thing, we
shall be able to understand the structure of our own mind, the
states of the various levels of our own being—where there is contradiction, blindness, self-assertiveness, brutality; we shall then
become aware of all the boiling, burning things within us. So let's
begin.

First of all, don't let us define what awareness is, because if we
do, each of us will give it a different meaning, a different definition. We shall find out what awareness means as we go along.

The moment you define what awareness is, you've already blocked yourself by words, by a conclusion. But if you say, "I'm going to find out what it means," then your mind becomes supple, elastic, and you can move along. So let's go into it. Don't complicate it, because as we begin to look into awareness, it will become more and more complex. But if you start with the complexity of it, you won't be able to see its extraordinary simplicity, and through this very simplicity to discover the diversity, contradictoriness, and dissimilarity that exist in awareness.

QUESTIONER: You mentioned awareness of things and states of mind. Does that mean that awareness always has an object, such as fear?

KRISHNAMURTI: We're going to find out. Look! I know nothing about it, right? I know nothing about awareness. I'm going to find out what it means, not what somebody tells me. First of all, am I aware, conscious, of outward things? The shape of the tree, the bird on the telegraph pole preening itself, the potholes in the road, the face opposite me. That is, just to look? First to look—to see! Or, do I see the image that I have about that bird, or tree, or the image that I have about the face I see in front of me? Is that somewhat clear? I see you—actually, visually—and also I have an image about you—you're old, young, nice looking, or you're dirty, you're this, you're that.

I see you not only visually, what you actually look like, but also, because I have known you, I have an image about you. Now that's part of awareness, isn't it? I'm aware of your face, your color, the scarf around your neck, the brown shirt—but I also have an image about you because I have known you—you have said pleasant or unpleasant things—I have built an image about you. That's part of awareness, isn't it? Of course!

Now, go a step further. I see you through the image which I have built about you. I see you—not only the brown shirt and so on, but also I see you through my image. Right? So actually I don't see you at all! That's part of awareness, isn't it? To realize that the image which is looking at you prevents the mind from looking at you directly. This is fairly simple. No?

Now, next move. By being aware of this, that awareness says,

I am really not looking at you at all—my image is looking at you! I am looking at you with my image. First of all, I am aware that I have an image, which I was not aware of before. Then I am aware how that image has come into being. Now, how has that image come into being? That image has come into being because you have hurt me, or have said pleasant things to me, flattered me, said "What a marvelous person you are," or said "For God's sake, become more intelligent," or whatever.

Through your verbal expression and the feeling which you have put into those words, and my reactions to those words and to those feelings, I have built an image about you—which is the memory that I have about you.

Q: But you form an image of someone even the first time you meet.

K: Yes, it can be in an instant. I don't like your face, or I do like your face. I like the perfume you have, or I don't like it, and so on. I've already built an image, instantly. So I am aware for the first time that I have an image about you. And also I am aware that this image has been put together by like and dislike. I am a German and you are a Frenchman and I don't like you and so on. So I am aware of the image I have built about you from my reactions to you. Shall we go on? Are you following the words or actually watching yourselves, watching the image you have about me or about someone else, how that image has been built? If you have a husband or a wife, you know very well how that image has been built; and are you aware of this image? Not whether you like it or dislike it. Because if you are aware and say "I like" or "I don't like," then you are adding to that image. Or you say, "I must get rid of that image." You're again adding to that image. But if you observe the image without any reaction—I wonder if you're following all this, is it too difficult?

This is a very complex process. Unless you follow very, very closely, you're going to miss the whole thing. Therefore, you have to pay attention. I am aware of your brown shirt and scarf and the color of your scarf. I am also aware that I look at you through the image I have built about you and that this image has been built through your words, through your gestures, or through my prejudice about you, or my like or dislike of you. That is part of awareness. And I also see, I am aware, that this image prevents me from looking at you directly, from coming into contact with you directly. Then I say to myself, "I must get rid of this image." Then the conflict begins, doesn't it? When I want to get rid of the image that I have built about you, to be free of it, because I want to come into closer contact with you, to see you directly, that is another form of reaction to the image.

So I am aware that I have an image which prevents me from looking, from observing exactly "what is," what exactly you are or exactly what I am. So I want to get rid of it, I want to be free of it, because this might be more profitable, more pleasurable, might bring me some kind of deeper, wider experience. And all this is part of awareness. The moment I want to get rid of that image, I am battling with it, which is conflict. So I am aware of what has happened now. I am aware of your brown shirt and the color of the scarf, I am aware of the image that I have built about you.

I am aware that this image is preventing me from coming directly in touch with you, seeing exactly what you are, or that the image which I have about myself prevents me from looking at myself. I want to get rid of that image because I've heard you say, self-knowledge is very important. Therefore, I don't want to have an image about myself. And when I want to get rid of it, then there is a conflict between the former image and a new image which I have created. So now I am in conflict. And if it is a conflict that promises a certain pleasure at the end of it, I want it to go on. And if it is a conflict that breeds pain, I want to get rid of it. So I am aware of the whole pattern of what is taking place.

I hope you are doing this with me—taking your own image, which you have about somebody, looking at it, being aware of it, as you are aware of the tent, its dimensions, structure, patches, holes, and so on. Similarly, you are aware of your image and what is implied by it. Now I'm in conflict. Either I am aware of that conflict as it is, or I want to alter that conflict into something which will give me more; or I am in conflict very superficially, just on the surface; or I am aware of the deeper layers of this conflict.

Awareness is not merely a superficial observance of conflicts within myself, but also through this awareness the deeper conflicts are being opened up. Then, if there is fear in that, I want to shut them all out, I don't want to look. So I run away from them through drink, drugs, women, men, amusement, entertainment, churches—all the rest of it. All that is part of awareness, isn't it?—the running away from fear, and giving importance to the things I have run to.

I am aware that I am lonely, miserable. I don't know a way out of it, or if I do know a way out, it's too difficult; therefore, I run away—to church, to drugs, to communism, to every form of entertainment. And because I have run away from the thing of which I am afraid, to something which helps me to escape, those things become tremendously important. So I'm attached to those things. It may be a wife, a family—whatever it is. Now all that is part of awareness, isn't it? I've begun very slowly—step by step—I watched your shirt, the color of your shirt, the color of your scarf, and have gone deeper and deeper until I found that I have a whole network of escapes. I haven't searched them out, I haven't analyzed them; by being aware, I have begun to penetrate deeper and deeper and deeper. Are you following all this?

Q: I don't follow. I see the point about being aware, but then comes a jump to inner escapes. Could you please go over it again?

K: Where is the jump?

Q: Between awareness and our escape, from, for instance, inner loneliness.

K: Oh, I thought I had made it clear. I have built an image about you and I was never aware of that image; and I become aware of it by observing outer things, by being aware of external things. Naturally from the external things I move to inner things. And there I discover I have an image about you. I went into it, that's clear, isn't it? Now, by becoming aware of that image, I find that I have built it in order to protect myself; or I have built it because you have said such brutal things to me that they remain in my memory, or you have said pleasant things which again remain in my memory. So there is the image which I have built, and I realize this image prevents me from looking deeper into my relationship with you.

Q: You mean, sir, that this awareness that you have is not just limited to one person but in every field?

K: Of course, I have images about everything—about you, about my wife, my children, my country, about God. [sound of jet aircraft overhead] Were you aware of the noise of that jet? Were you aware of your reaction to it? And the reaction was: I wish it would go away because I want to find out, I want him to talk more, it's preventing me from listening. Or did you just listen to that extraordinary thundering noise? When you listened to that thunder without any choice, you listened entirely differently, didn't you? No? You followed the thunder as it went further and further away. You listened to it and then you became aware of the different sounds of the river—didn't you?—of those children far away? But if you said, I don't like that sound because I want to listen here, I want to find out, then what has happened? Then you're in conflict, aren't you? You want to listen and you're prevented by that noise, so there is resistance to the noise and there is the desire to listen, to find out; therefore, there was conflict, and you were lost in that conflict. You neither listened to the thunder nor listened to what was being said. So let's proceed.

I have built an image about you, and now I see, I realize, am aware that this image prevents me from looking at you more clearly; and I want to get rid of that image because I want to see you more clearly, to understand you directly. So there is a conflict between the original image which I have about you and the new image I have in mind, which is to look at you. So there is conflict between the two. And as I don't know how to get rid of these images, I get tired, weary, and because I have no way of solving this, the conflict between the old image and the new image, I escape—and I have a network of escapes, of which I am slowly becoming aware: drink, smoking, incessant chatter, the offering of opinions, judgments, evaluations—dozens of escapes. I'm aware of these superficial escapes, and as I watch, I'm also beginning to discover the deeper layers of escapes. Are you following all this?

Q: In doing so, I lose touch with the observed.

K: I'm coming to that. You see, you are not actually doing it. If you are doing it step by step, you will soon discover the nature of the observer. So what has happened? Awareness has exposed a network of escapes, superficial escapes—and also with that awareness I see a deeper level of escapes—the motives, the traditions, the fears I have, and so on. So there I am. Beginning with the brown shirt and the scarf, I have discovered—awareness has shown—this extraordinary complex entity that I am—actually shown it!—not theoretically. That is, this awareness has actually shown "what is." Until now the observer has been watching all this taking place. I have watched that shirt, the color of the scarf, as though it were something outside me—which it is, right? Then I have watched the image which I have built about you. Then that awareness has shown the complexity of this image, and I'm still the observer of this image. So there is the image and the observer of that image (I am working and you are not!). So again there is the duality: the observer and the thing observed which is the image; and the dozens of images that I have (if I have them). And there are the superficial or deep escapes from the various forms of conflict which these images have caused. And there is still the observer watching them.

Now that awareness again goes on, deeper. Who is the observer?

Is the observer different from the images? Is not the observer another image? So one image, as the observer, observes the several images round him or in him. No? This observer is really the censor, the person who says "I like" or "I don't like" or "I like this image so I'm going to keep it" or "The other image I don't like so I want to get rid of it." But the observer is put together by the various images which have come into being through the reactions to them. Are you following all this?

Q: But all these images are in the observer.

K: Of course.

Q: But you say it is an image that sees another image?

K: Of course. I examined, I explored, until I came to the point where I said the observer is also the image, only he has separated himself and observes. Sir, please, this requires a great deal of real looking, not accepting anything that anybody says. This observer has come into being through the memories of various images and the reactions to them. Then the observer separates himself from the other images and says, "How am I to get rid of these images?" So this image is a permanent image! And this permanent image, which thinks it is permanent, says, "I want to get rid of all the other images because they really cause trouble, they really bring conflict," so it puts the blame on the other images. Whereas it is the observer-image that is the central cause of all this mischief.

Q: The image must get rid of itself.

K: Who is the entity that is going to get rid of it? Another image! It is really very important to understand this.

Q: Sir, if we look at these images, we see they are made of thought. If we look at the image of our self, the observer, we see that it builds up in the same way. I've got to this point.

K: Yes, you're perfectly right. We've got to that point. This awareness has revealed that there is a central image put together by the various other images, which has taken precedence. It is the censor, the evaluator, the judge, and it says, "I must get rid of all those others." So between it and the others there is a conflict. And we keep up this conflict all the time, and because we don't know how to resolve it, we have further escapes—either through neurosis or through conscious, deliberate escapes like drink, church, whatever it is. As this awareness pushes itself deeper— not, you push it—you ask: is the observer different from the other images? The other images are the result of judgments, opinions, conclusions, hurts, nationality—so the observer is the result of all the other images.

Q: We are afraid of such complexity.

K: But life is that! Therefore, you are afraid of life; therefore, you escape from life. You see, you're not really paying complete attention to this, and that's why it's so difficult to talk "against" something. Look, I have an image about you. That image has been put together by hurt, by like and dislike. That's a fact. That like and dislike has created another image in me—hasn't it?—not only the image about you but the other image, that I must not like or dislike, because it is absurd to like and dislike. Therefore, I have built an image which says, "I must not like or dislike," which is the outcome of building an image and seeing what is implied in it; this brings the other image into being.

Q: Some minds don't work that way at all. Mine doesn't.

K: All right. But we're talking about awareness, not how your mind works or my mind works. So the observer is the observed. There is the image of the observer; between the observer and the various images he has around him, there is a division, a separation, a time interval, and hence he wants to conquer them, he wants to subjugate them, he wants to destroy them. He wants to get rid of them, and hence there is a conflict between the observer and the observed. Right? And he says, "As long as I have conflict, I must be in confusion." So he says, "I must get rid of this conflict." The very desire to get rid of that conflict creates another image. Follow all this very closely. Awareness has revealed all this, revealed the various states of my mind, revealed various images, the contradictions between the images, the conflict, the despair of not being able to do anything about it, the escapes, the neurotic assumptions, and so on. All that has been revealed through cautious, hesitant awareness; and there is awareness that the observer is the observed. Please follow this! It is not that there is a superior entity which is aware that the observer is the observed, but this awareness has revealed the observer as the observed. Not, who is aware! Are you following all this?

You know, this is real meditation.

Now we can proceed. Now what takes place when the observer realizes that he is the observed? He has realized it not through any form of intellectual concept, idea, opinion, enforcement; he has realized this whole structure through this awareness—by being aware of the color of the shirt, the scarf, and moving, moving, deeper and deeper.

Q: I am extremely sorry to interrupt, but there's an important question that I don't understand, and that is, you say awareness sees that the observer is the observed. Now, does that mean that he is the actual observed or the reaction to the observed?

K: I don't quite understand your question, sir.

Q: Well, you say that the observer is the observed.

K: I don't say it.

Q: All right, awareness discovers that. You said that.

K: I did.

Q: So, here I have an image of you, let's say, and then awareness discovers that I am that observed, the observed which is the image. Do you mean that the observer is the image of you that he sees, or is he a reaction to that image?

K: Of course, he is the reaction to that image.
   (Someone else asks, "Could you explain this a little more?")

K [to first questioner]: Would you explain it, sir?

Q: Well, if you ask me to say something, I will.

K: Go ahead. You stand up, or come here—whatever you like.

Q: The speaker uses the words, that it is seen that the observer is the observed. Now we have been talking about things that are observed. A tree, that is the observed. Does the speaker mean that awareness sees that I am that tree? No. He says that what I see is not the tree, I see an image of the tree. So therefore, does he mean that I, as the observer, am that image of the tree, or does he mean that I as the observer am the reaction to that image of the tree? That was my question.

K: That's right, sir. You are the reaction to the image which you have created of that tree. If you had no image about that tree, there would be no observer.

Q: Sir, could one express this a little differently and say that the images that are built by like and dislike through innumerable associations about everything have also built up some conglomerate or aggregate that has formed the observer? Now, when we understand this inwardly, without trying to understand it, but are simply aware of it.

K: That's right, sir! That's perfectly right.

Q: Then you ask, "What happens?"

K: Now I'm going into that. This awareness has revealed that the observer is the observed; therefore, any action on the part of the observer only creates another image—naturally! If it is not realized that the observer is the observed, any movement on the part of the observer creates other series of images, and again he's caught in it. So what takes place? When the observer is the observed, the observer doesn't act at all. Go slowly, sir, go very slowly, because it's a very complex thing that we're going into now. I think this must be very clearly understood, otherwise we shan't get any further. The observer has always said, "I must do something about these images, I must get rid of them, I must suppress them, I must transform them, I must give them a different shape." The observer has always been active with regard to the observed. I observe that I dislike my wife—for various reasons—and the observer says, "I mustn't dislike her, I must do something about it," and so on. The observer is always active with regard to the thing observed.

Q: You mean that we are reacting all the time with all these images, constantly, in terms of like and dislike, and adding to them; that we are always doing this?

K: That's right; and this action of like and dislike on the part of the observer is called positive action.

Q: And that's what you mean when you say it is always active.

K: Yes, it is what is called positive action. I like, therefore I must hold on, or I don't like, therefore I must get rid of it. It's reacting, either passionately or casually. But when the observer realizes that the thing about which he is acting is himself . . .

Q: The gentleman over there wanted some more clarity on the observer and the observed. Now what you said then was that these images are not the actual things themselves. You don't know what they are, you only react to these images continuously. And when we see that, then this conflict between the observer and the observed ceases.

K: Sir, keep it very simple. I look at that brown shirt and the scarf. If I say, "I don't like that brown shirt and the scarf," or "I like that brown shirt and the scarf," I've already created an image, which is a reaction.

Q: And that stores up in the past, in memory.

K: That's right. Now, can I look at that brown shirt and the scarf without like and dislike, which is not to react to it but merely to observe? Then there is no image. You've got it? Have you got that very simple thing? The like and dislike is the result of my culture, my training, my tendency, my inclination, which already has an image which says, "I don't like that shirt," or "I like that shirt." So, the like and dislike and the past training—culture, inherited tendency—all that has created the image. That is my central observer, that is the observer put together by dislike and so on. That observer is obviously always separate from the thing he observes; and this awareness has revealed that the observer is the observed.

Q: The observed—do you mean by that the image which the mind has built up?

K: That's right. You've got it. Then, when the observer is the observed image, there is no conflict between himself and the image. He is that! He is not separate from that. Before, he was separate and took action about it, did something about it, reacted to it. But when the observer realizes he is that, there is no like or dislike. Sir—examine yourself.

Q: The observer is creating all the other images.

K: I'm not going to go back into that, sir. We have gone into it sufficiently. You understand what we have said so far, that between the observer and the observed, between the image which the observer has created about himself and the images which he has created about various things, there is a separation, a division, and hence, between himself and them, there is a conflict of like and dislike and reaction. And he is always doing something about it. Now, when the observer realizes he is the observed—the images—then conflict ceases. That is, when I realize I am fear—not, that there is fear and "me" separate from that fear—then I am that fear; I can't do anything. Follow this closely. Because, what am I to do? I am part of that fear. I am not separate from fear. Therefore, I can look at that fear without any form of escape. I am that fear, I am that pain which I have now in the tummy or my leg, or whatever it is. I am that fear. So I don't rebel against it or accept it or run away from it—it is there. So all action which is the outcome of the reaction of like and dislike has come to an end. You follow? Now what has happened?

Q: There is neither the observer nor the observed.

K: That's it. There is an awareness which is becoming more and more—I'm using "more and more" not in the sense of time—acute, sharp, intense.

Q: Not wasting energy.

K: That's right. It's becoming tremendously alive, it is not bound to any central issue, or to any image. And it is becoming intensely aware. From that intensity there comes a different quality of attention. Right?

Q: And this intensity has no direction and no purpose?

K: Watch it, you don't have to ask me, watch it yourself. The moment there is a choice in this awareness, then there is a direction directed by the observer. But when the whole pattern, when this whole structure has been understood, conflict has come to an end. And therefore, the mind—because the mind is this awareness—has become extraordinarily sensitive, highly intelligent! Because sensitivity goes with intelligence—there is no intelligence without sensitivity, physical as well as psychological. So the mind has become highly intelligent and sensitive, because that intelligence is not put together by any conflict.

In this awareness, because it has exposed everything very clearly, there has been no choice—choice only exists when there is confusion—and so this awareness has removed every form of conflict. Therefore, there is clarity. And this clarity is attention. Don't agree, please! This requires actual doing, not just agreeing! When there is this attention, in which there is no observer nor observed, this attention is intelligence. In this attention there is no conflict whatsoever; therefore, there is no demand for anything. And this attention has its own activity, its own action. So there is an action which is not born out of the observer. When the observer acts, his action is always separate. Look, we cannot go further into this unless you have actually done it—unless you actually do it. Then you will find that attention, being intelligence, is beauty and love—which the "separate observer" tried to imitate. And then the mind has no limit.

Breaking the Mirror

QUESTIONER: We can learn more from each other than by listening to K. Why don't you encourage people to hold group discussions on particular topics and have organized activities to facilitate dialogues and discussions?

KRISHNAMURTI: Are you listening to K? Or are you listening to yourself? K is saying: listen to yourself, see how conditioned you are—not, I am telling you that you are conditioned, but by listening to yourself, you learn infinitely more than by listening to a lot of other people, including K. But when you listen to K, he is not instructing you. He is putting up a mirror in front of you to see yourself. And when you see yourself very clearly, you can break the mirror, and the man who holds up the mirror.

So do we see ourselves clearly?

If we depend on relationship or on dialogue, associations, and institutions to teach us, to help us, to make things clear—what we are—then we depend. And when we depend on others, whatever it is, institutions, encounter groups, small groups, and so on, what are you learning? And what do you mean by learning? Please, this is again a very serious question. Learning, as we know it, is accumulating knowledge. I have learned about myself—that I am all this, all the pain, the misery, the confusion, the extraordinary travail of life—I am all that. I have learned it. That is, somebody has told me, or I have learned about myself. So learning, as far as we know it now, is accumulating knowledge about ourselves. And K says knowledge is the very root of disorder.

Go slowly.

Knowledge is necessary in the field of technology, in daily life, but psychologically knowledge is the very root of disorder, because knowledge is the past. Knowledge is always limited, because it is based on experience, hypothesis, conclusions, a chain—it is a constant addition of these; therefore, it is very limited. So can I look at myself without my previous knowledge or conclusion? You understand my question? I have looked at myself all yesterday, or a few hours yesterday, and I find that I am this, that, the other thing; I am depressed by it or elated by it. All that is going on. That becomes yesterday's knowledge. And with that knowledge I observe myself again. We do this. So knowledge is bringing about constant, psychologically mechanical repetition. And if you go into the matter very carefully with scientists, they are also beginning to discover that knowledge is a hindrance in certain areas of discovery.

So you are not learning or discovering anything from K. You are the storehouse of past history. That is a fact. You are the history of mankind. And if you know how to read that book, you don't have to depend on anybody, on discussions, or relationship, or organized groups and all that kind of thing. I am not saying you should not discuss, you should not have relationship, you should not have this or that. All that one is pointing out is that as long as you depend for your understanding of yourself on others, then you are lost. You have had leaders, haven't you? Religious leaders, political leaders, every kind of specialist who will tell you what to do, how to raise your children, how to have sex.

You have had every kind of leader for the last hundred thousand years or more. And where are you at the end of it? Do ask these questions, please. We are what we are because we have depended on others—somebody to tell us what to do, what to think, which means we are being programmed all the time. And to understand ourselves, there is every opportunity through relationship, through discussions, but if you depend on them, you are lost. Is this clear, this question? Not that you must agree with the speaker. But see the consequences of depending on others, depending on governments to bring order in this chaotic world, depending on a guru, depending on a priest, whether it is the pope or the local priest.

So the issue is really this: one is the storehouse of all mankind. One is the rest of mankind, and if one looks at that very closely, with a great deal of hesitation and affection, then you begin to read what you are, and then there is a flowering. But if you depend—then you live with pain and anxiety and fear.

Q: But even if we have no separate identity, we have got to have some form of government, surely?

K: Of course. Some form of government which is not based on separative governments.

Q: Who are going to be the politicians?

K: Oh, you see we want to organize it right away! First, sir, begin with ourselves, not what kind of governments to have, who the prime minister and chief treasurer will be. First, let's begin with ourselves. If all of us in this marquee really felt this in their heart, in their blood, we would have different governments in the world. We would put an end to wars.

Look, we are only pointing out one thing—our brains are conditioned. Whatever is conditioned is limited. Whatever is conditioned is separated, and this separation, this conditioning, is causing havoc in the world, which is a fact. And to stop that havoc, one must begin with oneself, not how to organize a new government. Am I conditioned? Am I thinking about myself endlessly from morning till night? In meditation, in exercise, in doing all kinds of things. I am more important than anybody else. I want all my desires fulfilled. I want to be somebody, recognized, so I am occupied with myself. The scientist may be occupied with his experiments, but he is also occupied with himself. He is also ambitious, wants a marvelous position, to be recognized by the world, get the Nobel Prize. I know some of them. One didn't get the Nobel Prize and the other did—you ought to see the fellow who didn't get it, how upset, bitter, and angry he was. You know, just like you and me, and everybody else.

So, sirs and ladies, if you really want to live on this peaceful earth, you have to begin very near, which is yourself.

Q: You talk about violence and freedom. But you say very little about law. Why is that? No civilized society can exist without laws. And laws sometimes have to be backed by force, which means violence. What do you do when terrorists hold hostages? Do you let them be killed, or storm the building? Where does freedom come into all this?

K: What is law? Doesn't it mean order, basically? A society establishes certain laws, whose purpose is to bring about order. But those very laws are broken by cunning people, by criminals who employ excellent lawyers. Now where does law, order begin? In the courts, with police superintendents and the intelligence service? Where does order begin? Please ask. Society is in disorder. This is a fact. Corrupt, immoral, and almost chaotic. And governments are trying to bring order in all that. We, you and another—we live in disorder—confused, uncertain, seeking our own security, not only our own but the security of one's family and so on. Each one is creating, through isolation, disorder. And where is law? With the police officer? With the lawyers? I have met several of them. They will protect a murderer, it is their job. A criminal pays them enormous sums.

Where is order, law in all this? So shouldn't we first face disorder? That is a fact, that we live in disorder and society is in disorder, governments are in disorder. If you have talked to some of the politicians, prime ministers, high up in the hierarchy of government, each one is after power and position, while holding on to, identifying with, certain concepts, ideologies, and all the rest of it. Each of us is working separately for himself. We will come together in a great crisis like war. But the moment the crisis is over, we are back to our old pattern.

So I am just suggesting this. If law means complete order, wouldn't you begin to find out whether you can live in complete order without any confusion? Put this question to yourself. So that there is no contradiction, saying one thing, doing another, thinking one thing and acting in another way. As long as we live in disorder, society and governments will be in disorder.

———

Words
and
Meanings

———

As indicated in the introduction, Krishna-murti has stressed his need to use "old words" in new ways in order to convey what he has to say. The following list, which is neither definitive nor authoritative, has been made in order to give a number of examples where his usage of words departs significantly from their dictionary definitions. It is preceded by a number of statements by him on the need to free oneself from the conditioning effects of language.

Words

UNFORTUNATELY WE ARE SLAVES to words and we are trying to reach something that is beyond words. To uproot, shatter the words and to be free of words gives an extraordinary perception, vitality, vigor.

—

This is not a matter that can be lightly dismissed, because the word—the symbol, the idea—has an extraordinary grip on the mind. We are talking of bringing about a mutation in the mind and for that there must be the cessation of the word[;] . . . now if the word is removed, what have you left? The word represents the past, does it not? The innumerable pictures, images, the layers of experience are all based on the word, the idea, memory. . . . [T]ake a word like *God*. The word *God* is not God; and one will come upon that intensity, that immeasurable something, whatever it may be, only when the word is not, when the symbol is not, when there is no belief, no idea.

—

You see, we use a word like *painful* and the very word prevents you from going into the problem. You know at the word *Swiss* the Swiss person is thrilled, as is the Christian at the word *Christ* and the Englishman at the word *England*. We are slaves to words, to symbols and ideas.

—

To comprehend every experience, every state of mind, the "what is," the actual fact, the actuality, one must not be a slave to words. The naming of it, the word, arouses various memories; and these memories impinge on the fact, control, shape, offer guidance to the fact, to the "what is."

—

Every word, thought, shapes the mind, and without understanding every thought, the mind becomes a slave to words and sorrow begins.

—

Every form of image, word, symbol must come to an end for the flowering of meditation . . . but the habit of the word, the emotional content of the word, the hidden implications of the word, prevent the freedom from the word. Without this freedom you are a slave to words, to conclusions, to ideas.

—

Can one listen without the word interfering? You say to me, "I love you," but what happens there? The words do not mean anything at all; but there may be a feeling of relationship which has not been brought about by the response of thought to the words; there may be a direct communication. So the mind, being aware that the word is not the thing, that the word, which is thought, interferes, listens freely, without prejudice—as it does when you say "I love you."

—

Words are a means of communication, but if particular words cause a neurological or psychological reaction in us, then it becomes very difficult to communicate.

—

When you call yourself a jealous person, for example, immediately you have blocked further inquiry, you have stopped penetrating into the whole problem of jealousy. Similarly there are many people who say they are working for brotherhood, yet everything they do is against brotherhood; but they don't see this fact because the word *brotherhood* means something to them and they are already persuaded by it; they don't inquire any further and so they never find out what are the facts, irrespective of the neurological or emotional response which that word evokes.

—

To know or experience immortality, or for the experiencing of that state, there must be no ideation. One cannot think about immortality . . . there is a great deal involved in this. The mind must be entirely quiet, without movement backward or forward, neither delving nor soaring. That is, ideation must entirely cease. And that is extremely difficult. That is why we cling to words like the *soul, immortality, continuity, God*—they all have neurological effects, which are sensations. And on these sensations the mind feeds; deprive the mind of these things, it feels lost. So it holds on with great strength to past experiences, which have now become sensations.

Is it possible for the mind to be so quiet—not partially, but in its totality—as to have direct experience of that which is unthinkable, of that which cannot be put into words?

—

The word *God* awakens all kinds of neurological and psychological reactions, and we are satisfied.

—

Take the word *love*. What an extraordinary neurological influence the word itself has on us!

—

The word has an extraordinary importance for most of us. The word *God*, the word *communist*, the word *negro* have an immense, emotional, neurological content. In the same way the word *jealousy* is also weighted. Now, when the word is put aside, there is a feeling that remains. That is the fact, not the word. And to look

at the feeling without the word requires freedom from all condemnation and justification.

Sometime when you are jealous, angry, or more especially
when you are enjoying yourself about something, see if you can
distinguish the word from the feeling, whether the word is all-
important or the feeling. Then you will find that in looking at the
fact without the word, there is an action which is not an intellectual process; the fact itself is operating, and therefore, there is no
contradiction, no conflict.

Meanings

———

Conditioning

QUESTIONER: You have talked a great deal about conditioning and have said that one must be free of this bondage, otherwise one always remains imprisoned. A statement of this kind seems so outrageous and unacceptable! Most of us are very deeply conditioned, and we hear this statement and throw up our hands and run away from such extravagant expression, but I have taken you seriously—for, after all, you have more or less given your life to this kind of thing, not as a hobby but with deep seriousness—and therefore, I should like to discuss it with you to see how far the human being can uncondition himself. Is it really possible, and if so, what does it mean? Is it possible for me, having lived in a world of habits, traditions, and the acceptance of orthodox notions in so many matters—is it possible for me really to throw off this deep-rooted conditioning? What exactly do you mean by conditioning, and what do you mean by freedom from conditioning?

KRISHNAMURTI: Let us take the first question first. We are conditioned—physically, nervously, mentally—by the climate we live in and the food we eat, by the culture in which we live, by the whole of our social, religious, and economic environment, by our experience, by education, and by family pressures and influences. All these are the factors which condition us. Our conscious and unconscious responses to all the challenges of our environment—intellectual, emotional, outward and inward—all these are the action of conditioning. Language is conditioning; all thought is the action, the response of conditioning.

Knowing that we are conditioned, we invent a divine agency which we piously hope will get us out of this mechanical state. We either postulate its existence outside or inside ourselves—as the atman, the soul, the Kingdom of Heaven which is within, and who knows what else! To these beliefs we cling desperately, not seeing that they themselves are part of the conditioning factor which they are supposed to destroy or redeem. So not being able to uncondition ourselves in this world, and not even seeing that conditioning is the problem, we think that freedom is in heaven, in moksha, in nirvana. In the Christian myth of original sin and in the whole Eastern doctrine of samsara, one sees that the factor of conditioning has been felt, though rather obscurely. If it had been clearly seen, naturally these doctrines and myths would not have arisen. Nowadays the psychologists also try to get to grips with this problem, and in doing so condition us still further. Thus the religious specialists have conditioned us, the social order has conditioned us, the family which is part of it has conditioned us. All this is the past which makes up the open as well as the hidden layers of the mind. En passant, it is interesting to note that the so-called individual doesn't exist at all, for his mind draws on the common reservoir of conditioning which he shares with everybody else, so the division between the community and the individual is false: there is only conditioning. This conditioning is action in all relationships—to things, people, and ideas.

Q: Then what am I to do to free myself from it all? To live in this mechanical state is not living at all, and yet all action, all will, all judgments are conditioned—so there is apparently nothing I can do about conditioning which isn't conditioned! I am tied hand and foot.

K: The very factor of conditioning in the past, in the present, and in the future, is the "me" which thinks in terms of time, the "me" which exerts itself; and now it exerts itself in the demand to be free; so the root of all conditioning is the thought which is the "me." The "me" is the very essence of the past, the "me" is time, the "me" is sorrow—the "me" endeavors to free itself from itself, the "me" makes efforts, struggles to achieve, to deny, to become. This struggle to become is time in which there is confusion and the greed for the more and the better. The "me" seeks security, and not finding it, transfers the search to heaven; the very "me" that identifies itself with something greater in which it hopes to lose itself—whether that be the nation, the ideal, or some god—is the factor of conditioning.

Q: You have taken everything away from me. What am I without this "me"?

K: If there is no "me," you are unconditioned, which means you are nothing.

Q: Can the "me" end without the effort of the "me"?

K: The effort to become something is the response, the action, of conditioning.

Q: How can the action of the "me" stop?

K: It can stop only if you see this whole thing, the whole business of it. If you see it in action, which is in relationship, the seeing is the ending of the "me." Not only is this seeing an action which is not conditioned, but also it acts upon conditioning.

Q: Do you mean to say that the brain—which is the result of vast evolution with its infinite conditioning—can free itself?

K: The brain is the result of time; it is conditioned to protect itself physically, but when it tries to protect itself psychologically, then the "me" begins, and all our misery starts. It is this effort to protect itself psychologically that is the affirmation of the "me." The brain can learn, can acquire knowledge technologically, but when it acquires knowledge psychologically, then that knowledge asserts itself in relationship as the "me" with its experiences, its will, and its violence. This is what brings division, conflict, and sorrow to relationship.

Q: Can this brain be still and only operate when it has to work technologically—only operate when knowledge is demanded in action, as for example, in learning a language, driving a car, or building a house?

K: The danger in this is the dividing of the brain into the psychological and the technological. This again becomes a contradiction, a conditioning, a theory. The real question is whether the brain, the whole of it, can be still, quiet, and respond efficiently only when it has to in technology or in living. So we are not concerned with the psychological or the technological; we ask only, can this whole mind be completely still and function only when it has to? We say it can, and this is the understanding of what meditation is.

—

Q: If I may, I should like to continue where we left off yesterday. You may remember that I asked two questions: I asked what is conditioning and what is freedom from conditioning, and you said let us take the first question first. We hadn't time to go into the second question, so I should like to ask today, what is the state of the mind that is free from all its conditioning? After talking with you yesterday, it became very clear to me how deeply and strongly I am conditioned, and I saw—at least I think I saw—an opening, a crack in this structure of conditioning. I talked the matter over with a friend, and in taking certain factual instances of conditioning, I saw very clearly how deeply and venomously one's actions are affected by it. As you said at the end, meditation is the emptying of the mind of all conditioning so that there is no distortion or illusion. How is one to be free of all distortion, all illusion? What is illusion?

K: It is so easy to deceive oneself, so easy to convince oneself of anything at all. The feeling that one must be something is the beginning of deception, and, of course, this idealistic attitude leads to various forms of hypocrisy. What makes illusion? Well, one of the factors is this constant comparison between what is and what should be, or what might be, this measurement between the good and the bad, thought trying to improve itself, the memory of pleasure, trying to get more pleasure, and so on. It is this desire for more, this dissatisfaction, which makes one accept or have faith in something, and this must inevitably lead to every form of deception and illusion. It is desire and fear, hope and despair, that project the goal, the conclusion to be experienced. Therefore, this experience has no reality. All so-called religious experiences follow this pattern. The very desire for enlightenment must also breed the acceptance of authority, and this is the opposite of enlightenment. Desire, dissatisfaction, fear, pleasure, wanting more, wanting to change, all of which is measurement— this is the way of illusion.

Q: Do you really have no illusion at all about anything?

K: I am not all the time measuring myself or others. This freedom from measurement comes about when you are really living with what is—neither wishing to change it nor judging it in terms of good and bad. Living with something is not the acceptance of it: it is there whether you accept it or not. Living with something is not identifying yourself with it either.

Q: Can we go back to the question of what this freedom is that one really wants? This desire for freedom expresses itself in everybody, sometimes in the stupidest ways, but I think one can say that in the human heart there is always this deep longing for freedom which is never realized; there is this incessant struggle to be free. I know I am not free; I am caught in so many wants. How am I to be free, and what does it mean to be really, honestly free?

K: Perhaps this may help us to understand it: total negation is that freedom. To negate everything we consider to be positive, to negate the total social morality, to negate all inward acceptance of authority, to negate everything one has said or concluded about reality, to negate all tradition, all teaching, all knowledge except technological knowledge, to negate all experience, to negate all the drives which stem from remembered or forgotten pleasures, to negate all fulfillment, to negate all commitments to act in a particular way, to negate all ideas, all principles, all theories. Such negation is the most positive action; therefore, it is freedom.

Q: If I chisel away at this, bit by bit, I shall go on forever, and that itself will be my bondage. Can it all wither away in a flash, can I negate the whole human deception, all the values and aspiration and standards, immediately? Is it really possible? Doesn't it require enormous capacity, which I lack, enormous understanding, to see all this in a flash and leave it exposed to the light, to that intelligence you have talked about? I wonder, sir, if you know what this entails. To ask me, an ordinary man with an ordinary education, to plunge into something which seems like an incredible nothingness. . . . Can I do it? I don't even know what it means to jump into it! It's like asking me to become all of a sudden the most beautiful, innocent, lovely human being. You see I am really frightened now, not the way I was frightened before; I am faced now with something which I know is true, and yet my utter incapacity to do it binds me. I see the beauty of this thing, to be really completely nothing, but . . .

K: You know, it is only when there is emptiness in oneself, not the emptiness of a shallow mind but the emptiness that comes with the total negation of everything one has been and should be and will be—it is only in this emptiness that there is creation; it is only in this emptiness that something new can take place. Fear is the thought of the unknown, so you are really frightened of leaving the known, the attachments, the satisfactions, the pleasurable memories, the continuity and security which give comfort. Thought is comparing this with what it thinks is emptiness. This imagination of emptiness is fear, so fear is thought. To come back to your question—can the mind negate everything it has known, the total content of its own conscious and unconscious self, which is the very essence of yourself? Can you negate yourself completely? If not, there is no freedom. Freedom is not freedom from something that is only a reaction; freedom comes in total denial.

Q: But what is the good of having such freedom? You are asking me to die, aren't you?

K: Of course! I wonder how you are using the word *good* when you say what is the good of this freedom? Good in terms of what? The known? Freedom is the absolute good and its action is the beauty of everyday life. In this freedom alone there is living, and without it how can there be love? Everything exists and has its being in this freedom. It is everywhere and nowhere. It has no frontiers. Can you die now to everything you know and not wait for tomorrow to die? This freedom is eternity and ecstasy and love.

Knowledge

Knowledge is the residue of experience, the accumulated knowledge of the race, of society, of science. All the accumulation of human endeavor as experience, scientifically or personally, is knowledge.

—

Psychological knowledge, the knowledge that I want this, that I have experienced this, I believe this, this is my opinion, all the psychological residue of one's experiences, and the experiences of mankind stored up in the brain, from that there is thought, and that thought is always limited, and any action born from that must inevitably be limited and therefore not harmonious but contradictory, divisive, conflicting, and so on.

—

This is what we mean by psychological knowledge. That is, I have built up, psychologically, a great deal of information about my wife or girlfriend. I have built up this knowledge about her correctly or incorrectly, depending on my sensitivity, my ambition, greed, envy, and all that, depending on my self-centered activity. So that knowledge is preventing actual observation of the person, who is a living thing. I never want to meet that living thing because I am afraid. It is much safer to have an image about that person than to see the living thing.

—

We know we are afraid, that we are lonely, that we have great sorrow, we know we are depressed, anxious, uncertain, unhappy, trying to fulfill, to become, to get something all the time—all that is the movement of knowledge. We are asking whether that psychological knowledge, which always overcomes, distorts, technological knowledge, can come to an end.

—

We carry a great burden of knowledge, of hurts, insults, various emotional, psychological reactions, various forms of experience. Our brain is burdened with all that, not only with academic knowledge, but the whole psychological world which is loaded with knowledge, the known. And as long as thought is working in that field, can there be freedom? . . . [W]hen the brain is totally free from all accumulated psychological knowledge, then there is the mind.

Attachment

What is attachment? Why are we attached to something or other—to property, money, to wife, to husband, to some foolish conclusion, to some ideological concept? Why are we so attached? Let us inquire into it together. And the consequences of attachment.

If I'm attached to you, if the speaker is attached to you as an audience, think what his state of brain must be. He's frightened he may not have an audience. He becomes nervous and almost apoplectic. And he is attached to exploiting people, to having a reputation. So the consequences of attachment, if you observe it very closely, whether it be to a wife, husband, a boy or a girl, an idea, a picture, a memory, an experience, the consequences are that it breeds the fear of losing. And out of that fear there is jealousy. How jealous we are. Jealous of those in power—you follow? All the jealousy. And from jealousy there is hatred. Of course, jealousy is hatred. And when you are attached, there is always suspicion, secrecy. Haven't you noticed all this? It's so common in the world. And can you, if you are attached to something or some idea, some person, can you end it now? That is death. Which means, can you live with death all day long? Ah, think of it, go into it. You will see the greatness of it, the immensity of it. That is, not commit suicide, we are not talking of that silly stuff, but to live with that, ending all sense of attachment, all sense of fear. Which means having a brain that is acting but never having direction, purpose, all the rest of it. Acting. That is to live with death every second, never collecting, never gathering, never giving anything a continuity. Sirs, you don't know; if you do it, you will see what it means. That is real freedom. And from that freedom there is love. Love is not attachment. Love is not pleasure, desire, fulfillment.

—

I am attached to you, you are nice looking, you give me pleasure, sex or companionship, or whatever, and I am greatly attached to you. That attachment is the past[,] . . . I am attached to you through that pleasure, and that attachment is a remembrance, because the next time you are not there, I say, "Oh, I wish you were here." So attachment is a remembrance[,] . . . there is no attachment when there is the living present.

Pleasure

What is pleasure? How does it come about? You see a sunset, and seeing it gives you great delight. You experience it . . . and that experience leaves a memory of pleasure, and tomorrow you will want that pleasure repeated. . . . [T]his repetition takes place, as you can observe, when thought thinks about it and gives it vitality and continuity. It is the same with sex, the same with other forms of physical and psychological pleasure. Thought creates the image of that pleasure and keeps on thinking about it.

—

The next question is: how can one not think about this? . . . [J]oy is not pleasure. You can't think about joy, or rather you can think about it and reduce it to pleasure, but the thing that is called joy, ecstasy, is not the product of thought. Haven't you noticed that when there is a great burst of joy, you can't think about it the next day, and if you do, it has already become pleasure? . . . [I]s it possible for an incident, whether it is painful or pleasurable, to end and not leave a mark on the brain? The mark on the brain is memory, and then when memory responds, its response is thought. . . . [T]here was that incident of the beautiful sunset, as you looked at it, there was great delight. You observed it, the colors, the light on the water, the various shades of the light in the cloud. Can you observe it without the word? The moment you use the word, that word has associations, and those associations are part of the memory. When you say how extraordinary it is, you have already gone away from looking, from observing, from seeing the sunset. So can you look at the sunset without the word? Which means to look at it completely, with complete attention, not comparing it with the sunset you saw in California or another part of the world, or saying to your friends how lovely it is, but just to look, without the word. That means: to look with complete attention.

Then you will find, if you so look, that very perception prevents a memory being formed about that sunset. Which doesn't mean that you haven't any joy, delight in it.

———

Pleasure is not only the instant pleasure, the instant desire, but also the demand for the continuity of a psychological pleasure which I have had. In all that is included thinking. In all that there is the process of recognition, the word, the demand for a continuity[,] . . . there is the instant pleasure of eating a fruit, and a second later I want more. The "more" of anything is not the actual moment.

———

Thinking about that experience of yesterday, whether it was gazing at the lovely tree, the sky and the hills, or your sexual enjoyment, is pleasure.

———

Pleasure is the movement of thought after the actuality has gone, which is entirely different from that which is enjoyable. You enjoy. If you like food, you enjoy food, but thought comes in and says I must have the same kind of food tomorrow. Then the habit begins. Then thought says I must break the habit, so all the conflict begins. Whereas if you are fond of food, taste it, enjoy it, and end it there. You understand? Not say I must have it tomorrow or this evening. So in the same way to observe your wife, your husband, everything, without registering and therefore giving it a continuity, then that gives the brain a tremendous freedom; you have established order where it should be orderly, and you have cleared away all disorder in relationship, because then there is no image between you and her.

Image

By an image the speaker means a symbol, a concept, a conclusion, an ideal. These are all images—that is what I should be—I am not this, but I would like to be that. That is an image projected by the mind in time, that is, into the future. So that is unreal. What is real is what is actually taking place now in your mind. Can we go on from there?

We are asking why the mind creates an image. Is it because in the image there is security? If I have a wife, I create an image about her—the very word *wife* is an image. And I create that image because although the wife is a living, changing, vital human entity, and to understand her requires much more attention, greater energy, if I have an image about her, it is much easier to live with that.

First of all, haven't you an image about yourself, that you are a great man or not a great man, that you are this or that? When you live with images, you are living with illusions, not with reality[,] . . . why does the mind, your mind, make images? Is it because in images there is security, however false the images are? . . . [T]he image is the projection of thought . . . and thinking is the response of memory stored up in the brain as knowledge. Knowledge comes from experience[,] . . . you have experience, you remember that experience as knowledge, and that knowledge remembered projects thought[,] . . . but knowledge is always limited, there is no complete knowledge about anything. So thought is always limited.

—

The mind must find out how to empty its content—that is, have no image, and therefore no observer. The image means the past or the image which is taking place now or the image which I shall project into the future. So no image, which means no formula, idea, principle—all that implies image. Can there be no formation of image at all? You hurt me or give me pleasure, and therefore, I have an image of you. Is it possible to have no image formation when you hurt me or give me pleasure? For example, when you insult me, to be completely watchful, attentive, so that it doesn't leave a mark?

—

When I have no image about you and you have no image about me, it is only then that whatever you say leaves no mark—which doesn't mean I am isolated, or have no affection, but the registration of hurts, insults, all those movements of thought, has come to an end. Which means, at the moment of insult, to be completely attentive, with all your senses.

—

Psychologically, inwardly, not to have a single shadow of image, then nobody can hurt you.

—

What we mean by looking at a tree with innocence is to look at it without the image. In the same way, you have to look at violence without the image that is involved in the word itself.

—

For most of us the relationships we have with one another are mechanistic. I mean by mechanistic the image created by thought about you and about me.

—

We mean by right relationship a state of mind and heart in which all the machinery that builds the image has come to an end, so that there is complete harmony not only within oneself but with another.

———

To have no image about yourself does not mean that you are lost, that you become insecure, uncertain. On the contrary, when you have an image about yourself, that image creates uncertainty.

———

To worship another is to worship oneself. The image, the symbol, is a projection of oneself.

———

The image is the projection of past experience. The past experience has brought about this image, and according to that image I act, which is the future.

———

When you understand desire, this involves not only the object outside but also the psychological projection of an image.

———

Any form of image you have about another, or about yourself, prevents the beauty of relationship.

Thinking

What is thinking? Can you think without memory? You cannot think without memory. Then what is memory? Go on. Put your brains into it. Remembrance? A long association of ideas, a long bundle of memories? Then what is memory? I remember the house I lived in. I remember my childhood. What is that? The past. Right? The past is memory. And you don't know what will happen tomorrow, but you can project what might happen or might not happen. That is the action of memory in time.

So what is memory? How does memory come about? This is all so simple. Memory cannot exist without knowledge. If I had a car accident yesterday, that accident is remembered. But previous to that remembrance, there was the accident. The experience of the accident becomes knowledge, then from that knowledge arises memory. If I had no accident, there would be no memory of an accident. Also, you can imagine other people's accidents.

So knowledge is based on experience. But experience is always limited. I can have more experience, more varieties of experience, not only physical or sexual, but also so-called inward experience of some illusory god and so on. So experience, knowledge, memory, thought, experience being always limited. I can't experience the immensity of the order of the universe. But I can imagine it.

Experience is limited, and therefore, knowledge is limited, whether in the future or now. Because knowledge is always being added to, more and more. Scientific knowledge is based on that. From before Galileo and ever since, it has been added to, added to, added to. So knowledge is always limited, whether now or in the future. So memory is limited. So thought is limited. This is where the difficulty is. Thought is limited. Thought has invented gods, saviors, rituals, Lenin and Marx and Stalin. So thought, whatever it does, noble or ignoble, religious or nonreligious, virtuous or not virtuous, moral or immoral, is still limited, whatever thought does. Are we together in this?

Hurt

What is hurt? Don't go verbally but actually go into yourself, look at yourself. Psychologically you are hurt, your parents hurt you when you were a child, your friends hurt you when you were a child. Then the school hurt you by saying, "You must be as clever as your brother," or your uncle, or your headmaster, or whoever it was. And then at college you must pass exams, and if you fail, you are hurt. And if you don't get a job, you are hurt. Everything in the world is put together so that it hurts you. Our education, which is so rotten, hurts you. So you are hurt. Do you actually realize that you are hurt? And see the results of being hurt—that you want to hurt others? From that arises anger, resistance, you withdraw, become more and more inwardly separate. And the more you are inwardly separate, and withdraw, the more you are hurt. So you build a wall around yourself and pretend, but always within the wall. These are all the symptoms.

So you are hurt. And if you really, deeply realize that you are hurt, not only at the conscious level but deep down, then what will you do? Now, how does this hurt take place? Because you have an image about yourself. If I have an image about myself always sitting on a platform talking to an audience—thank God, I don't—and if the audience disapproves or doesn't come, my image about myself is hurt. The fact is that as long as I have an image about myself, that image is going to be hurt. That's clear, isn't it? Now is it possible to live without a single image? Which means no conclusions, no prejudices—all these are images. And the moment that you insult me, which is when you say something contrary to the image I have about myself, then you hurt me. Now if at that moment when you are saying something that is harmful, hurtful, I am aware and I give my total attention to what you are saying, then no registration takes place. It is only when there is inattention that the registration of hurt or flattery takes place. So when somebody says you are a fool, can you at that moment give your total attention? If you do, there is no hurt. The past hurts have gone in that attention. Attention is like a flame that burns out the past and the present hurt. Have you got this?

Attention

QUESTIONER: You have said that when one gives complete attention to a problem, then the problem flowers and withers away. Can you explain this further?

KRISHNAMURTI: There is, say, the problem of conflict. Now can you watch your conflict and give it complete attention? Please just listen to it for a few minutes. Listen. You have a problem, which is conflict. Can you look at it, not only listen to the problem, the tones, the content, the subtleties of the problem, can you look at it without trying to resolve it, without trying to give it any direction, without any motive? When you have a motive, it gives it a direction, and therefore, you are distorting the problem. So can you sensitively be aware of conflict? Not act upon it, because you are part of that conflict. You are conflict. So if you act upon it, you further create more conflict. So look at that conflict—the little one and the whole human conflict, the personal and the global, look at it. Listen to its story, don't you tell what the story is, let it tell you the story. Like a child sitting on your lap whom you love, who is telling you a story. You don't interrupt the child. You are not rude to it, you want him to tell you all about it.

In the same way, let this conflict tell you all about it, only you have to have ears to listen to it, not only with hearing of the ear but also hear inwardly the nature of it. Can you so listen to it, giving your whole attention to it, without any effort? When you are with a child telling you a story, you are not making an effort and saying, "I must control myself, I must be more patient." You are listening because you love that child. Listen in the same way, and then you will see the problem flowers, grows, shows its whole content. And when it has shown all its content, it passes away, it is finished. You understand? That is, the flowering and the withering of a problem, which doesn't involve time. It is only the impatient mind that brings in time, that says, "I must solve this." But a mind that is listening very carefully, sensitively, alert to all its tiny, very subtle movements, when you listen to the problem, when you give your complete attention to it—and you cannot give complete attention if you have a motive, if you have a direction, if you say, "I must do this"—then nothing will happen. But if you give your total attention, the problem shows itself fully and so dissolves. Like a flower, in the morning the bud is there, in the evening it has withered.

Vulnerability

When reason no longer has the capacity to protect you through explanations, escapes, logical conclusions, then there is complete vulnerability, utter nakedness of your whole being, there is the flame of love.

———

As this is a conversation, a dialogue between you and the speaker, we ought to be vulnerable—that is, not have any defense, any resistance, but be willing to expose ourselves completely, not only to the problem, but to what is involved in the problem, giving our whole attention to it.

———

Do you see the necessity of being open and vulnerable? If you do not see the truth of that, then you will again surreptitiously build walls around yourself.

———

The essence of sensitivity is to be vulnerable[;] . . . to be vulnerable inwardly means not having any resistance, not having any image, any formula.

Perception

What does perception mean? Can I have perception if I am attached to my position, my wife, my property? . . . [W]e are saying that total perception can take place only when in your daily life there is no confusion[;] . . . if I am in fear, my perception will be very partial . . . but in investigating, observing, going into fear, understanding it profoundly, in delving into it, I have perception. . . . [P]erception can take place only when there is no division between the observer and the observed.

———

All the sensory impressions, the impressions that are recorded consciously and unconsciously, the various images, conclusions, prejudices, all that is involved in perception[,] . . . and when I meet you, I turn on attention and the images emerge. This is what we call perception . . . but order is perception of things as they are—perception of what you are, not my conclusion of what you are. I say perception is seeing things as they are, and I cannot see things as they are if I have a conclusion. In conclusion, therefore, there is disorder.

—

There is a totally different kind of energy when there is pure perception, which is not related to thought and time.

—

Is there a perception of violence which will end that violence instantly? . . . [P]erception is action, and when you see a snake, you act instantly. There is no saying, "Well, I will act next week," there is immediate response because there is danger.

—

What matters is to observe your own mind without judgment— just to look at it, to watch it, to be conscious of the fact that your mind is a slave and nothing more. Because that very perception releases energy, and it is this energy that is going to destroy the slavishness of the mind[,] . . . we are concerned only with perceiving what is. And it is the perception of "what is" that releases the creative fire[,] . . . the urgency behind the right question, the very insistence of it, brings about perception. The perceiving mind is living, moving, full of energy, and only such a mind can understand what truth is.

—

If thought continues, the mind is never quiet, and it is only when the mind is completely quiet that there is the possibility of perception. See the logic of it—that is, if my mind is chattering, comparing, judging, saying, "This is right, this is wrong," then I am not listening to you.

—

Perception implies complete attention—the nerves, the ears, the brain, the heart, everything is of the highest quality[,] . . . it is the self which makes for fragmentation. In the absence of self there is perception. Perception is doing, and that is beauty.

—

There can be perception only when it is not tinged by thought; when there is no interference from the movement of thought, there is perception, which is direct insight into a problem. Does perception originate in the mind? Yes, when the brain is quiet.

Insight

What is insight? That is, to perceive something instantly which must be true, logical, sane, rational. And that insight must act instantly[,] . . . to have an insight, for example, into the wounds, hurts that one has received from childhood. . . . [T]he hurt is the image that you have created about yourself. . . . [N]ow to have an insight into all that without analysis, to see it instantly, and through the very perception of that insight, which demands all your energy and attention, the hurt is dissolved.

—

What is insight, then? We are saying insight can take place only when knowledge has come to an end and there is pure observation without any direction . . . and that insight is not the result of constant examination, constant analysis, examining day after day; it is sudden cessation of all knowledge and seeing something directly. That insight brings about a fundamental change in the very brain cells themselves that carry memory.

—

When you have an insight into attachment, you go behind the word, you go behind your reactions of asserting and not asserting, you see, observe, how the mind has built up this whole process of attachment. And you can only observe it when you don't want to discard it. You can only observe when you see that the observer is that thing which you are seeing. The observer has created the attachment and then disassociated himself from it and tries to change, control, shape, deny, alter, go beyond, and all the rest of it. Now when you have an insight of that kind, out of that insight comes intelligence.

—

This constant insight without a formula, without a conclusion that puts an end to that insight, is creative action. It is astonishingly beautiful and interesting how thought is absent when you have an insight. Thought cannot have an insight. It is only when the mind is not operating mechanically in the structure of thought that you have an insight. . . . [H]aving an insight and never drawing a conclusion from it so that you are moving constantly from insight to insight, action to action, is spontaneity[,] . . . a mind that is free has insight every minute; a mind that is free has no conclusion and is therefore nonmechanical. . . . [T]here is security in insight, not in conclusion.

—

Insight is not a remembrance, is not a calculated, investigated result; it is not a process of recording and acting from that, and it is no longer the activity of thought, which is time. Insight therefore is the action of a mind that is not caught in time.

Passion

When you fall in love with someone, you are in a great state of emotion, which is the effect of that particular cause; and what I am talking about is passion without a cause. It is to be passionate about everything, not just about something, whereas most of us are passionate about a particular person or thing; and I think we must see this distinction very clearly. In the state of passion without a cause there is intensity free from all attachment; but when passion has a cause, there is attachment, and attachment is the beginning of sorrow. . . . [W]hen there is a passion for something, for a person, an idea, some kind of fulfillment, then out of that passion, there comes contradiction, conflict, effort[,] . . . please, may I suggest that you just listen: don't try to achieve this state

of intensity, this passion without a cause. If we can listen attentively, with that sense of ease which comes when attention is
not forced through discipline, but is born of the simple urge to
understand, then I think we shall find for ourselves what this passion is[,] . . . I think the ending of sorrow is related to the intensity
of passion. There can be passion only when there is total self-
abandonment.

One is never passionate unless there is a complete absence of
what we call thought[,] . . . that passion has nothing whatsoever
to do with enthusiasm. It comes only when there is a complete
cessation of the "me," when all sense of "my house," "my property," "my country," "my wife," "my children" has been left behind.
You may say, "Then it is not worth having." Perhaps for you it is
not. It is worthwhile only if you really want to find out what is
sorrow, what is truth, what is God, what is the meaning of this
whole ugly and confusing business of existence. If that is what
you are concerned with, then you must go into it with passion—
which means that you cannot be tethered to your family. You
may have a house, you may have a family, but if you are psychologically tethered to them, you cannot go beyond.

—

When there is no wastage of energy, then there is passion.

—

For most of us, passion is employed with regard to one thing
only, sex; or you suffer passionately and try to resolve that suffering. But I am using the word *passion* in the sense of a state of mind,
a state of being, a state of your inward core—if there is such a
thing—that feels very strongly, that is highly sensitive—sensitive
alike to dirt, squalor, poverty, to enormous riches and corruption,
and to the beauty of a tree, a bird, the flow of water, a pond
that has the evening sky reflected on it. To feel all this intensely,
strongly, is necessary. Because without such passion, life becomes
empty, shallow, without much meaning. If you cannot see the
beauty of a tree and love that tree, if you cannot care for it intensely, you are not living[,] . . . we are talking of a passion without motive. . . . [T]o understand what is true, you must have
passion.

—

Remaining with suffering, not escaping from it, brings passion. Passion means the complete abandonment of the "me," the self, the ego—and therefore a great austerity, the austerity of great beauty[;] . . . without that inward quality of passion which is the outcome of great understanding of sorrow, I don't see how beauty can exist.

—

A mind that is passionate is inquiring, searching, looking, asking, demanding, not merely trying to find, to relieve its discontent, some object in which it can fulfill itself and go to sleep[;] . . . the passion to find out, to inquire, to search, to understand, can only come about when the "me" is absent.

—

The perception of truth demands passion, intensity, an explosive energy, not a mind that is crushed through fear, discipline, and all the horrors of cultivated virtue; these are all the partial pursuits of the broken mind. When you see this thing, then your whole being is in it. Only the mind that is passionate, that knows the passion of freedom—such a mind alone can find that which is measureless.

—

One has to come upon this passion which is neither lust nor has any motive. Is there such passion? There is such passion when there is an end to sorrow.

Action

If we realize that all thinking is inadequate to solve our problems—and realize this not as a logical conclusion, not as an aphorism, but as a truth, as a law that thought is inadequate because thought is a fragment, and as such has created the world and divided the world. So all that is seen, and also there is the realization that you are the world and the world is you—fundamentally, basically, because wherever you go, there is suffering, tears, misery, confusion, hunger, starvation—it is the common ground of humanity.

So you are the world and the world is you. And when you realize that thought, mankind's thought, is inadequate to solve the human problem of living, existence, relationship, fear, all that, then what happens? . . . [N]ow, how do you realize that truth? Is it an intellectual acceptance, a theory that one has proposed, and you accept it as a theory? Do you make an abstraction, an ideal of the statement that you are the world and the world is you and that thought is inadequate, or do you live with it? . . . [W]e say: live with it, look at it, hold it like a jewel, don't you tell it what to do, look at that jewel which you have; it will tell you what to do.

But we are so eager to tell it what to do. You understand? You read a story, a thriller, it's all written down, you don't have to tell it what should happen. So in the same way you have here the most extraordinary jewel—to realize that you are the world and the world is you, and that thought is totally, absolutely inadequate to solve our human problems of relationship—to see that and to live with it every minute of the day, then you will find out what correct action is.

Learning

When do you learn? Learning is different from knowing, isn't it? Accumulating knowledge is different from learning. The moment I have learned, it has become knowledge. After I have learned, I add more to it. This process of adding we call learning, but that is merely the accumulation of knowledge. I am not against such accumulation, but we are trying to find out what the act of learning is. The mind is really learning only when it is in a state of not knowing. When I do not know, I am learning.

—

Knowledge is not learning. Learning is always in the active present. Knowledge is always of the past, and we live on the past, are satisfied with the past, . . . but if you are learning, that means "learning all the time," which is an active present, learning every minute. Learning by watching and listening, learning by seeing and doing—then you will see that learning is a constant movement without the past.

—

Now we are going to find out if there is a different action of learning, which is not accumulation of knowledge. Let me put it differently. First there is experience, and from experience knowledge, from knowledge memory, and the response of memory is thought. Then thought acts, from that action you learn more, so you repeat the cycle. This is the pattern of our life. And we are saying that form of learning will never solve our problems because it is repetition. It is so obvious we haven't solved them[,] . . . now is there another form of learning? Learning not in the context of knowledge, but a different form—of nonaccumulative perception-action.

—

When you are learning, your mind is always attentive and never accumulating—therefore, there is no accumulation from which you judge, evaluate, condemn, and compare[,] . . . watching, looking, seeing, listening are all parts of learning[,] . . . to learn about yourself, all previous knowledge about yourself must come to an end.

Meditation

Now, what is meditation? As we do not know what it is, we have no idea how to begin. So we must approach it with an open mind, mustn't we? You must come to it with a free mind which says, "I do not know," and not with an occupied mind which is asking, "How am I to meditate?" Please, if you will really follow this—not hold on to what I am saying but actually experience the thing as we go along—then you will find out for yourself the significance of meditation.

We have so far approached this problem with an attitude of asking how to meditate, what systems to follow, how to breathe, what kind of yoga practices to do, and all the rest of it, because we think we know what meditation is, and that the "how" will lead us to something. But do we know what meditation is, actually? I do not, nor, I think, do you. So we must both come to the question with a mind that says "I do not know"—though we may have read hundreds of books and practiced many yoga disciplines. You do not actually know. You only hope, you only desire, you only want, through a particular pattern of action, of discipline, to arrive at a certain state. And that state may be utterly illusory; it may be only your own wish. And surely it is; it is your own projection, as a reaction from the daily existence of misery.

So the first essential is not how to meditate, but to find out what meditation is. Therefore, the mind must come to it without knowing—and that is extremely difficult. We are so used to thinking that a particular system is essential in order to meditate—either the repetition of words, as prayer, or the taking of a certain posture, or fixing the mind on a particular phrase or picture, or breathing regularly, making the body very still, having complete control of the mind; with these things we are familiar. And we believe these things will lead us to something which we think is beyond the mind, beyond the transient process of thought. We think we already know what we want, and we are now trying to compare different ways to find the best one.

That issue of "how" to meditate is completely false. Rather, can I find out what meditation is? That is the real question. It is an extraordinary thing, to meditate, to know what meditation is, so let us find out.

Surely meditation is not the pursuit of any system, is it? Can my mind entirely eliminate this tradition of a discipline, of a method?—which exists not only here, but also in India. That is essential, isn't it? Because I do not know what meditation is. I know how to concentrate, how to control, how to discipline, what to do; but I do not know what is at the end of it, I have only been told "If you do these things, you will get it," and because I am greedy, I carry out those practices. So can I, to find out what meditation is, eliminate this demand for a method?

The very going into all this is meditation, isn't it? I am meditating the moment I begin to inquire what meditation is, instead of how to meditate. The moment I begin to find out for myself what meditation is, my mind, not knowing, must reject everything that it knows—which means, I must put aside my desire to achieve a state. Because the desire to achieve is the root, the base, of my search for a method. I have known moments of peace, quietness, and a sense of "otherness," and I want to achieve that again, to make it a permanent state—so I pursue the "how." I think I already know what the other state is, and that a method will lead me to it. But if I already know what the other is, then it is not what is true, it is merely a projection of my own desire.

My mind, when it is really inquiring what meditation is, understands the desire to achieve, to gain a result, and so is free from it. Therefore, it has completely set aside all authority. Because we do not know what meditation is, and no one can tell us, my mind is completely in a state of "not knowing," there is no method, no prayer, no repetition of words, no concentration—because it sees that concentration is only another form of achievement. The concentration of the mind on a particular idea, hoping thereby to train itself to go further by exclusion, implies, again, a state of "knowing." So if I do not know, then all these things must go. I no longer think in terms of achieving, arriving. There is no longer a sense of accumulation which will help me to reach the other shore.

So when I have done that, have I not found what meditation is? There is no conflict, no struggle; there is a sense of not accumulating—at all times, not at any particular time. So meditation is the process of complete denudation of the mind, the purgation of all sense of accumulation and achievement—that sense which is the very nature of the self, the "me." Practicing various methods only strengthens that "me." You may cover it up, you may beautify it, refine it; but it is still the "me." So meditation is the uncovering of the ways of the self.

And you will find, if you can go deeply into it, that there is never a moment when meditation becomes a habit. For habit implies accumulation, and where there is accumulation, there is the process of the self asking for more, demanding further accumulation. Such meditation is within the field of the known, and has no significance whatsoever except as a means of self-hypnosis.

The mind can only say "I do not know"—actually, not merely verbally—when it has wiped away, through awareness, through self-knowledge, this whole sense of accumulation. So meditation is dying to one's accumulations, not achieving a state of silence, of quietness. So long as the mind is capable of accumulating, then the urge is always for more. And the "more" demands the system, the method, the setting up of authority—which are all the very ways of the self. When the mind has seen the fallacy of that completely, then it is in a constant state of "not knowing." Such a mind can then receive that which is not measurable and which only comes into being from moment to moment.

PART III

Action through Inaction

As indicated in the introduction, Krishnamurti may be said to give a special kind of answer to the question "What is action?" What follows are three examples of forms of inaction from which action arises. They are preceded by a passage on "observing" that stresses the need for awareness that the inner psychological processes and discoveries involved are common to all of us, such awareness being necessary to avoid self-centered, "lopsided" introspection. They are followed by a few final thoughts under the title "On Issues Often Discussed."

Observing

————

WHEN WE ARE OBSERVING ourselves, we are not isolating, limiting ourselves, becoming self-centered—because we are the world and the world is us. This is a fact. And when we, as human beings, examine the whole content of our consciousness, of ourselves, we are really inquiring into the human being as a whole—whether one lives in Asia, Europe, or America.

So it is not a self-centered activity. That must be very clear. When we are observing ourselves, we are not becoming selfish, becoming more and more neurotic, lopsided. On the contrary, when we are looking at ourselves, we are examining the whole human problem, the human problem of misery, conflict, and the appalling things that man has done to himself and others.

It is very important to understand this fact, that we are the world and the world is us. We may have superficial mannerisms, superficial tendencies that are different, but basically all human beings throughout this unfortunate world go through confusion, turmoil, violence, despair, agony.

There is common ground on which we all meet.

So when we observe ourselves, we are observing human beings. I hope this is clear and that we do not make this observation into some neurotic, lopsided, selfish affair, as most people are apt to do.

Staying with "What Is"

———

I WANT TO SEE what actually takes place when there is an enormous crisis and the mind realizes that any form of an escape is a projection into the future, and remains with the fact of the crisis without any movement. The *fact* of the crisis is immovable. Can the mind remain with that immovable fact and not move away from it?

Let us make it very simple. I am angry, furious, because I have given my life to something and I find someone has betrayed that and I feel furious. That fury is all energy. I haven't acted upon that energy. It is a gathering of all my energy which is expressed in anger, in fury. So then not to translate, not to hit out, not rationalize, just to hold it[;] . . . look, I want to get at something here. Say my son dies. I am not only in despair, but I am in profound shock, with a deep sense of loss which I call sorrow. My instinctual response is to run away, to explain, to act upon it. Now I realize the futility of that, and I don't act. I won't call it despair, sorrow, or anger, but I see the fact is the only thing—nothing else. Everything else is nonfact.

Now what takes place then? That's what I want to get at. If you remain with what you had called despair without naming, without recognizing it, if you remain with it totally without any movement of thought, what takes place? . . . [C]an I face the fact without any sense of hope or despair, all that verbal structure, and just say, "I am what I am"? I think then some kind of explosive action takes place—if I can remain *there[,]* . . . when my son is dead, that is an immovable, irrevocable fact. And when I remain with that, which is also an immovable, irrevocable fact, the two facts meet. So what takes place then?

—

Let's first remain with the fact and let it tell its whole story. I am attached, say, to my psychological wound. I like that wound, I hold on to it, it gives me some anchor around which I can worry. Can I watch that wound which I have received from childhood and let the whole thing flower, without *you* making it flower or *my* denying, controlling, loving, holding on to it? Let that thing flower and see what happens. . . . [C]an you remain with an illusion, let it flower, not say, "What is an illusion, what is not an illusion, how can I get rid of it, isn't it good to have a little bit of illusion?" But just say, "Yes, I see I am in illusion which thought has created psychologically and which is totally unreal."

—

Look, there is this fact. I am confused. There is an awareness of that confusion, and to remain with it, not twist it, not try to go beyond it, is to be silent with that confusion . . . not trying to do something about it. Remain with it in silence, let it tell you, you are part of it, be open, be sensitive. It will flower, and out of that comes clarity.

—

Can the mind remain with the fact? Now what *is* the fact? Please listen carefully. The fact of suffering—is it the *word* that has created the feeling or is it *actual* suffering? Is the mind facing suffering or does it face what it calls suffering because of a word called suffering? The word is not the thing. And is the suffering a word or a reality? So I must find out whether the mind is caught in words. The words may be an escape.

So I have to find out whether the mind is capable of being free from the word and therefore capable of looking at "what is" without the word; because words play an extraordinarily important part in our life—Christian, German, a black man, a white man—you immediately have an image. . . . [T]hen if it is not the word that is stimulating the feeling, can the mind remain with the fact of that feeling and not move away from it? When you do that, you have tremendous energy—which was previously dissipated. And when you have that energy, then what is suffering? *Is* there suffering then? . . . [W]hen the mind remains totally with the fact and not the word, with the fact of that feeling of great sorrow *without any escapes*, out of that comes passion[,] . . . can the mind look at hurt without a trace of saying, "I want to hit back, I want to build a wall around myself so I am never hurt again"—remaining with the fact, not with the word? Then you will see you have great energy to go beyond it. It doesn't then exist at all. Do do it, please.

—

The man who remains with "what is" and never moves away from it bears no marks.

—

What is important is not to escape, not to make an effort, just to remain with "what is."

—

Try remaining with the feeling of hate, envy, jealousy, with the venom of ambition. For, after all, that's what you have in daily life, though you may want to live with love or with the word *love*. Since you have the feeling of hate, of wanting to hurt somebody with a gesture or a burning word, see if you can stay with that feeling. Can you? . . . [Y]ou will find it amazingly difficult. Your mind will not let the feeling alone. It comes rushing in with its remembrances, its associations, its dos and don'ts, its everlasting chatter. Pick up a piece of shell. Can you look at it, wonder at its delicate beauty, without saying how pretty it is or what animal made it? Can you look without the movement of the mind? Can you live with the feeling behind the word, without the feeling that the word builds up? If you can, then you will discover an extraordinary thing, a movement beyond the measure of time, a spring that knows no summer.

—

If you remain with the fact of anything, especially with the fact of sorrow, and don't let thought wander or explain it away, but completely identify yourself with it, then there is tremendous energy, and out of that energy there is the flame of passion.

—

Remain with suffering without the word, without the desire to go beyond it, so that you are observing it without the observer, so that there is no division between you and the thing which you call sorrow. Because the moment there is a division between you as the observer, the thinker, and the observed, which is suffering, there is not only conflict but the desire to go beyond, to escape from it.

—

You have done something, which is a fact, and you feel guilty, that is a fact, and you stay with it. You stay with it like a jewel, a rather unpleasant one, but it is still a jewel[,] . . . when you stay with it, it begins to flower; then it shows itself fully, all the implications of guilt, its subtlety, where it hides. It is like a flower blooming.

—

Usually in our relationship we are attached to a person. Can we stay with the fact that we are attached and watch it? And let the whole nature of attachment reveal itself . . . let the thing that you are watching tell its story, rather than *you* tell it what it *should* be.

—

To stay with fear means not to escape, not to seek its cause, not to rationalize or transcend it. To stay with something means that. Like staying with looking at the moon—just look at it.

—

When you begin to be choicelessly aware of your self-interest, to stay with it, to study, learn about it, observe all its intricacies, then one can find out for oneself where it is necessary and where it is completely unnecessary[,] . . . also, watching, staying with things that disturb you, things that please you, staying with things that are abstract, all the imaginations, all the things that the brain has put together, including God.

———

Is it possible to look and stay with the whole movement of fear? I mean by staying with it to observe without any movement of thought entering into my observation?

———

When you are greedy, envious, is that envy different from you? Or you *are* envy. Of course you are. But when there is a division between envy and you, then you want to do something about it, control, shape, yield to it, and so on. And when there is a division between you and that quality, there must be conflict.

But the *actuality* is that you *are* envy. That is a fact. You are not separate from it. You are not separate from your face, your name, your bank account, your values, your experience, your knowledge. So when one realizes this truth, that you are not separate from that which you feel, which you desire, pursue, or fear, there is no conflict. Therefore, you *stay with that;* you don't move away from it, you *are* that. Therefore, there is tremendous energy to look at it[,] . . . you stay with it as though you are holding a precious jewel in your hand; you look at it, watch it, play with it; there is such a sense of release, of freedom.

———

There is an ending to sorrow if one remains with it completely, holds it as one would a precious baby, holds it in one's heart, one's brain, stays with it. And you will find this extraordinarily arduous, because we are so conditioned that the instinctive reaction is to get away from it. But if you can remain with it, you will find there is an ending—totally—to sorrow. Which doesn't mean that you become insensitive to it.

Asking but Not Answering Fundamental Questions

———

WE ARE USED TO thinking in terms of time, of *becoming* something. Being confused, in sorrow, without love, being full of the bitterness of frustration in the everlasting struggle to become something, we say, "I must have time to be free of all that," and we never ask ourselves, "Can I be free, not in time, but immediately?" It is always necessary to ask fundamental questions and never seek answers to them, because to fundamental questions there are no answers. The question itself, with its depth and clarity, is its own answer[,] . . . the known is made up of the things that you have learned, have been taught. It is made up of your desire to be prime minister, or rich, and so on. And can the mind, being the result of the known, do anything else but move everlastingly in the field of the known? Can this movement in the field of the known come to an end without any incentive? Because if there is an incentive, that is also the known.

Surely as long as there is this movement of the known in the field of the known, it is impossible for the mind to know the unknown. So can that movement of the known come to an end? That is the problem. If you really put that simple question without trying to find an answer, without wanting to "get somewhere," and if you are in earnest because it is a fundamental question for

you, then you will find that the movement of the known comes
to an end. That is all. With the cessation of the mind as the
known, with its freedom from the movement of the known, there
is the coming into being of the unknowable, the immeasurable,
and in that there is an ecstasy, a bliss.

—

You have to ask a question and not seek an answer because the
answer will invariably be according to your conditioning, and to
break down the conditioning, you must ask without seeking an
answer.

—

I feel it is very important to ask fundamental questions and to
keep on asking them without trying to find an answer. Because
the more you persist in asking such questions, demanding, inquiring, the sharper and more aware the mind becomes[,] . . . the
whole endeavor of self-improvement is the result of conditioning.
And can the mind be totally free from such conditioning? If you
really put that question to yourself attentively without seeking an
answer, then you will find the right one, which is not that it
is possible or impossible—but something entirely different takes
place.

—

We know the mind is mechanical. Then the next response is:
how am I to stop it? In putting this question, the mind is again
mechanical. That is, I want a result, there is a means, and I want
to use that. What has happened? The "how" is the response of a
mechanical mind, the response of the old. . . . [T]here are two
different states of the mind, one pursuing the "how" and the other
inquiring and not seeking a result. Only the mind which inquires
will help us[,] . . . is your mind really inquiring to find out
whether the mechanical mind can come to an end? Can it? Have
you put that question? If you have, with what motive, intention,
purpose? That is very important. If you have put that question
with the motive that you want a result of which you are conscious, then you are back again in the mechanical process. If you

really put the question *without* the intention to find out what happens, if you inquire, you will find that your mind is not seeking a result, it is waiting for an answer. It is not speculating about an answer, not desiring, not hoping for one. It is waiting.

Look at this. I ask you a question. What is your response? Your immediate response is to think, to reason, to look, to find out a clever argument to reply[;] . . . that is, you are not answering, you are responding, giving reasons. In other words, you are *seeking* an answer. If you want to find out the answer to a question, the response, other than waiting, is mechanical. That is, the mind that waits for an answer to come is nonmechanical, because the answer is something you don't know—the answer which you *know* is mechanical. But if you face the question and *wait* for an answer, you will see that your mind is in an entirely different state. *The waiting is more important than the answer.*

Then the mind is no longer mechanical but in quite a different process. There is something quite different that, without being invited, comes into being.

—

It is only the mind that has accumulated knowledge and is held by it that has sorrow—not the sensitive mind, the inquiring mind, not the mind that is questioning, asking. Such a mind puts the question because it is a marvelous thing to do so without seeking an answer, because the question then unravels, it begins to open the doors and windows of your mind. And so through this questioning, watching, listening, your mind becomes extraordinarily sensitive.

—

To fundamental questions there is no absolute answer of "yes" or "no." What is important is to put a fundamental question, not to find an answer; and if we are capable of looking at that question without seeking an answer, then that very observation of the fundamental brings about understanding.

—

There is no answer to any problem, there is only an understanding of the problem.

—

There is a questioning which is merely to question, not trying to find an answer. That very questioning opens the door through which you can find out, look, observe, and listen.

—

If you put a question without wanting an answer, you will find the answer. But if you put the question hoping to find the answer, your answer will then be according to your conditioning.

—

Is it possible to live in this world with all the complications without a single shadow of conflict? You have planted this question in your brain; let it remain there, see what happens.

The Beauty of Not Knowing

BEING AFRAID OF DEATH, we go to doctors, try new medi-
cines, new drugs, and perhaps we may live for another
twenty or thirty years by doing so. But there it is, inevitably,
around the corner. And to face that fact—to *face* it, not to *think*
about it—requires a mind that is dead to the past, a mind that is
actually in a state of *not knowing*. . . . [T]he moment you think in
terms of hope or despair, you are again within the field of time,
of fear. To go through that very strange experience of dying,
not at the ultimate moment of physical death when one becomes
unconscious, or one's mind is dull, made stupid by disease or
drugs or accident, but to die to the many yesterdays in full consciousness, with full vitality and awareness—surely that does create a mind which is in a state of not knowing, and therefore of
meditation.

If you are asked a question of which you know nothing at all so
that you have no referent in memory, and if you are capable of
replying honestly that you do not know, then that state of not
knowing is the first step of real inquiry into the unknown. . . .
[S]o if I see the truth of that and actually put aside all the answers,
which I can do only when there is this immense humility of not
knowing, then what is the state of the mind? What is the state of

the mind which says, "I do not know whether there is God, whether there is love"? That is, when there is no response of memory. . . . [T]hat state in which the mind says "I do not know" is not negation. The mind has stopped searching completely; it has ceased making any movement, for it sees that any movement out of the known toward what it calls the unknown is only a projection from the known. So the state of a mind that is capable of saying "I do not know" is the only state in which anything can be discovered. . . . [C]an the man who says "I know," and whose mind is burdened with information, with encyclopedic knowledge, ever experience something which is not to be accumulated? He will find it extremely hard. When the mind puts aside totally all the knowledge that it has acquired, when for it there are no Buddhas, no Christs, no masters, no teachers, no religions, no quotations, when the mind is completely alone, uncontaminated, which means that the movement of the known has come to an end—only then is there a possibility of a fundamental change, of a tremendous revolution.

—

Only the mind which is capable of being in a state of not knowing—not merely as a verbal assertion but as an actual fact—is free to discover reality. But to be in that state is difficult because we are ashamed of not knowing. Knowledge gives us strength, importance, a center around which the ego can be active. The mind which is not calling upon knowledge, which is not living in memory, which is emptying itself totally of the past, dying to every form of accumulation from moment to moment—it is only such a mind that can be in a state of not knowing[;] . . . the man who understands himself seeks nothing, his mind is limitless, undesirous, and for such a mind the immeasurable can come into being.

—

What is love? You don't know. Is that state of not knowing—love?

—

The mind that lives in a state of not knowing is a free mind. . . . A mind that lives in the known is always in prison. Can the mind say "I do not know"? Which means the yesterday has ended. It is the "knowledge of continuity" which is the prison.

———

I am not against the accumulation of knowledge, but we are trying to find out what the act of learning is. The mind is really learning only when it is in a state of not knowing. When I do not know, I am learning.

———

Now can the mind free itself from the known, from the past, from all tradition, from all knowledge? And when it does, is not the mind in a state of not knowing? Being free from the known, is it not capable of understanding or experiencing the unknown, which is death?

———

Can the mind free itself from this urge to be secure? It can do so, surely, only when it is completely uncertain—not uncertain in opposition to security, but when it is in a state of not knowing and not seeking. After all, one can never find anything new so long as one's mind is burdened with the old, with all the beliefs, fears, and hidden compulsions which bring about this search for security.

On Issues Often Discussed

———

THE FEAR OF DEATH ceases only when the unknown enters your heart. Life is the unknown, as death is the unknown, as truth is the unknown.

———

To go inward very deeply, the outer must also be understood. The more you understand the outer—not merely the fact of the distance between here and the moon, technological knowledge, but the outward movements of society, of nations, the wars, the hate that there is—when you understand the outer, then you can go very deeply inwardly, and that inward depth has no limit.

———

When I understand myself, I understand you, and out of that understanding comes love.

———

The mind, seeing what is false, has put it aside completely—but not knowing what is true. If you already know what is true, then you are merely exchanging what you consider is false for what you imagine is true. There is no renunciation if you know what you are going to get in return. There is only renunciation when you drop something not knowing what is going to happen.

—

When the whole mind, including the brain, is empty of the known, then you will use the known when necessary but functioning always from the unknown, from the mind that is free of the known.

—

It is only when I do not know what God is that there is God.

—

The ending of that which is not good is goodness.

—

In becoming something there is great uncertainty, whereas in not becoming, which is to remain totally with that emptiness, is to be nothing, and is therefore complete security.

—

To be free of tomorrow is to live only in the active present.

—

To be willing to have nothing happening in the mind: that is supreme intelligence.

—

Freedom from the known can take place only when one has observed the whole phenomenon of working in the field of the known.

—

What takes place when there is no loneliness, when there is complete self-sufficiency, no dependency? When there is no dependency, what takes place? I love you, you may not love me. I love you—that's good enough. I don't want your response that you love me, I don't care. Like a flower, it is there for you to look at, to smell, to see the beauty of it. The flower doesn't say "Love me"—it is there. Therefore, it is related to everything. In that state of self-sufficiency—not in the ugly sense, but in the great depth and beauty of sufficiency—there is no loneliness, no ambition, that is really love. Therefore, love is related to nature. If you want it, there it is. If you don't want it, it doesn't matter. That's the beauty of it.

—

If I love my wife, I must also love everybody. When you really love, then pleasure, sex, and so on have a different quality.

—

You can know yourself only when you are unaware, when you are not calculating, not protecting, not constantly watching to guide, to transform, to subdue, to control. When you see yourself unexpectedly, that is, when the mind has no preconceptions with regard to itself, when the mind is open, unprepared to meet the unknown.

Appendix

———

SINCE KRISHNAMURTI'S DEATH, schools that seek to apply his approach to education have continued in India, the United States, and England.

The Brockwood Park School in England is residential, international, and coeducational and provides secondary and higher education for fourteen- to twenty-four-year-olds.

The Krishnamurti Centre accommodates adult guests who wish to study Krishnamurti's works in quiet surroundings, whether by the day, on weekends, or for a week or so.

The Krishnamurti Foundation Trust maintains the Krishnamurti archives and distributes books and audio and video recordings.

The following is the address for all three organizations:

> Brockwood Park
> Bramdean, Hampshire SO24 0LQ
> England

Additional contact information for these organizations is as follows:

> Brockwood Park School
>   Phone: (0) 1962 771 744
>   Fax: (0) 1962 771 875
>   E-mail: admin@brockwood.org.uk

The Krishnamurti Study Centre
Phone: (0) 1962 771 748
E-mail: kcentre@brockwood.org.uk

The Krishnamurti Foundation Trust
Phone: (0) 1962 771 525
Fax: (0) 1962 771 159
E-mail: kft@brockwood.org.uk

Source Notes

WITH A FEW EXCEPTIONS indicated below, readers wishing to consult the complete texts from which the extracts in this book have been taken will find them in the *Krishnamurti Text Collection, 1933–1985.* This CD-ROM, which contains material equivalent to two hundred average-sized books, is an invaluable source for the study of Krishnamurti. For extracts dated up through 1967, the complete texts can also be found in the volumes of *The Collected Works of J. Krishnamurti,* © 1991 Krishnamurti Foundation of America (referred to hereafter as *The Collected Works*).

FRONTISPIECE

"Don't accept . . . for yourself." From the talk at Saanen on July 28, 1978.
"You must . . . in spite of me." From a talk at Eerde in June 1927.
"If you . . . any teacher." From the talk at Auckland on March 31, 1934.

INTRODUCTION

"If you . . . any teacher." From the talk at Auckland on March 31, 1934.
"Whether I am . . . in daily life." From the talk at Bombay on March 12, 1961.
"The speaker . . . question." From the talk at Saanen on July 25, 1983.
"Words are . . . convenient meaning." From the talk at Ommen on August 2, 1930.
"As the majority . . . no value." From the talk at Ommen on July 31, 1930.
"To find out . . . or God." From the talk at Bombay on March 25, 1956.

PART I: THE CORE OF THE TEACHING

Listening

"I hope you will . . . how one listens." From the talk at Bombay on February 14, 1954, in *The Collected Works.*
"Can one listen . . . to find out." From the talk at Madras on January 6, 1971, in *Krishnamurti in India, 1970–71,* © 1971–1972 Krishnamurti Foundation Trust, Ltd.

"I think there is . . . thinking, resisting." From the talk at Bombay on March 6, 1955, in *The Collected Works*.

"I do not know . . . of the brain." From the tape of the talk at Saanen on July 17, 1980, © 1980 Krishnamurti Foundation Trust, Ltd.

Truth Is a Pathless Land

"To me there is . . . daily life." From the talk at Adyar on January 2, 1934.

"Truth is something . . . an extraordinary thing truth is." From the talk at Rajghat on December 25, 1952, in *The Collected Works*.

"The fact is . . . living is truth." From chapter 17 of *This Matter of Culture*, © Krishnamurti Foundation Trust, Ltd.

Is There Such a Thing as Truth Apart from Personal Opinion?

From the tape of the question-and-answer meeting at Ojai on May 8, 1980, © 1980 Krishnamurti Foundation Trust, Ltd.

There Is Only Infinite Watching

From the tape of the conversation with Mary Zimbalist and Ray McCoy at Brockwood Park on October 14, 1984, © 1984 Krishnamurti Foundation Trust, Ltd.

A Man Addicted to Knowledge Cannot Find the Truth

From the talk at Madras on November 16, 1947, in *The Collected Works*.

There Is No Technique

From the dialogue at Saanen on July 29, 1976, © 1976–1977 Krishnamurti Foundation Trust, Ltd.

You Have to Find Truth through the Mirror of Relationship

From chapter 7, part 2, of *The Wholeness of Life*, © 1978 Krishnamurti Foundation Trust, Ltd.

Human Beings Have Built in Themselves Images as a Fence of Security

From the talk on November 8, 1980, in *Sri Lanka Talks, 1980*, © 1980–1981 Krishnamurti Foundation Trust, Ltd.

The Burden of These Images Dominates Thinking, Relationships, and Daily Life

From the dialogue at Saanen on August 6, 1972, © 1972 Krishnamurti Foundation Trust, Ltd.

Freedom from Being a Slave to the Past

From the dialogue on August 8, 1965, in *The Collected Works*.

Thought Is Always Limited

From chapter 55 of *Commentaries on Living, First Series*, © 1956 Krishnamurti Writings Inc.

The Content of One's Consciousness Is One's Entire Existence
From the tape of the talk at Brockwood Park on September 8, 1973, © 1973 Krishnamurti Foundation Trust, Ltd.

One's Perception of Life Is Shaped by Concepts Already Established in One's Mind
From the tape of the talk at Saanen on July 14, 1974, © 1974 Krishnamurti Foundation Trust, Ltd.

One's Uniqueness as a Human Being Lies in Complete Freedom from the Content of One's Consciousness
From the tape of the talk at Brockwood Park on September 17, 1972, © 1972 Krishnamurti Foundation Trust, Ltd.

Choiceless Awareness
From the talk on July 24, 1977, in chapter 9, part 2, of *The Wholeness of Life*, © 1978 Krishnamurti Foundation Trust, Ltd.

Freedom Is Found in the Choiceless Awareness of Daily Existence and Activity
From the talk on February 10, 1971, in *Krishnamurti in India, 1970–71*, © 1971 Krishnamurti Foundation Trust, Ltd.

Thought Is Time
From the tape of the talk at Brockwood Park on September 9, 1973, © 1973 Krishnamurti Foundation Trust, Ltd.

Time Is the Psychological Enemy
From the tape of the talk at Saanen on July 15, 1984, © 1984 Krishnamurti Foundation Trust, Ltd.

In Observation One Begins to Discover the Lack of Freedom
From the talk at Poona on September 21, 1958, in *The Collected Works*.

A Radical Mutation in the Mind
From the tape of the question-and-answer meeting at Saanen on July 25, 1983, © 1983 Krishnamurti Foundation Trust, Ltd.

Total Negation Is the Essence of the Positive
From the talk at Rajghat on January 31, 1960, in *The Collected Works*.

The Division between the Thinker and the Thought, the Observer and the Observed
"Do please follow this . . . of 'what is.'" From the talk at Claremont College on November 17, 1968, in *1968 Talks with American Students*, © 1968 Krishnamurti Foundation Trust, Ltd.
"Then what is the function . . . what truth is." From the talk at Bangalore on January 30, 1971, in *Krishnamurti in India, 1970–71*, © 1971 Krishnamurti Foundation Trust, Ltd.
"Look at the sky . . . to love somebody." From the talk at Bangalore on January

31, 1971, in *Krishnamurti in India, 1970–71,* © 1971 Krishnamurti Foundation Trust, Ltd.

"Now let us examine . . . something totally different." From the talk at Saanen on July 22, 1971, in *The Awakening of Intelligence,* © 1973 Krishnamurti Foundation Trust, Ltd.

"How shall we proceed . . . love and beauty." From the talk at Saanen on July 25, 1968, in *Talks and Dialogues, 1968,* © 1969 Krishnamurti Foundation Trust, Ltd.

"If you can observe . . . wastage of energy." From the talk at Madras on January 10, 1971, in *Krishnamurti in India, 1970–71,* © 1971 Krishnamurti Foundation Trust, Ltd.

This Division between the Observer and the Observed Is an Illusion

From the talk on August 7, 1967, in *Talks and Dialogues, Saanen, 1967,* © 1968 Krishnamurti Foundation Trust, Ltd.

Breaking the Mirror

From the talk at Brockwood Park on September 1, 1983, © 1983 Krishnamurti Foundation Trust, Ltd.

Part II: Words and Meanings

Words

"Unfortunately . . . vigor." From the talk in London on May 2, 1961, in *The Collected Works.*

"This is not . . . no idea." Extracts from the talk at Saanen on July 14, 1963, in *The Collected Works.*

"You see . . . and ideas." From the talk at Saanen on July 25, 1961, in *The Collected Works.*

"To comprehend . . . 'what is.'" From the talk at Madras on January 29, 1964, in *The Collected Works.*

"Every word . . . sorrow begins." From *Krishnamurti's Notebook,* p. 191.

"Every form . . . to ideas." Extracts from *Krishnamurti's Notebook,* p. 204.

"Can one listen . . . 'I love you.'" From *Beyond Violence,* p. 171.

"Words are . . . to communicate." From the talk at Ojai on August 9, 1952, in *The Collected Works.*

"When you call yourself . . . that word evokes." From *This Matter of Culture,* p. 25.

"To know . . . put into words?" Extracts from the talk at Ojai on August 7, 1949, in *The Collected Works.*

"The word *God* . . . satisfied." From the talk at Madras on January 27, 1952, in *The Collected Works.*

"Take the word . . . on us!" From the talk at Banares on January 30, 1955, in *The Collected Works.*

"The word has . . . no conflict." From the talk in Paris on September 10, 1961, in *The Collected Works.*

Meanings

CONDITIONING
From *The Urgency of Change*, pp. 142–50.

KNOWLEDGE
"Knowledge is . . . knowledge." From the tape of the dialogue at Brockwood Park on September 12, 1972.

"Psychological knowledge . . . and so on." From the tape of the talk at Ojai on April 21, 1979.

"This is what . . . the living thing." From the tape of the question-and-answer meeting at Ojai on May 6, 1980.

"We know . . . come to an end." From the tape of the talk at Bombay on February 8, 1981.

"We carry . . . the mind." Extracts from the tape of the talk at Madras on January 11, 1981.

ATTACHMENT
"What is attachment . . . pleasure, desire, fulfillment." From the tape of the talk at Ojai on May 19, 1985.

"I am attached . . . the living present." Extracts from the tape of the dialogue at Saanen on August 1, 1974.

PLEASURE
"What is pleasure . . . thinking about it." Extracts from the tape of the talk at the University of Puerto Rico on September 17, 1968.

"The next question is . . . delight in it." Extracts from the tape of the talk at Sydney on November 25, 1970.

"Pleasure is . . . the actual moment." From the dialogue at Saanen on August 7, 1966, in *The Collected Works*.

"Thinking about . . . is pleasure." From the tape of the talk at Claremont College on November 17, 1968.

"Pleasure is the movement . . . between you and her." From the tape of the talk at Brockwood Park on August 29, 1976.

IMAGE
"By an image . . . is always limited." Extracts from the tape of the talk at Colombo on November 8, 1980.

"The mind must . . . leave a mark?" From the second conversation with Prof. J. Needleman in *The Awakening of Intelligence, Part I*.

"When I have no . . . all your senses." From the tape of the talk at Saanen on July 20, 1976.

"Psychologically . . . hurt you." From the tape of the question-and-answer meeting at Madras on January 7, 1981.

"What we mean . . . the word itself." From the talk at Bombay on February 22, 1967, in *The Collected Works*.

"For most of us . . . and about me." From the tape of the talk at Saanen on July 20, 1972.

"We mean by right . . . with another." From the tape of the talk in San Francisco on March 11, 1973.

"To have no image . . . uncertainty." From the tape of the talk in Madras on December 24, 1977.

"To worship another . . . of oneself." From *Commentaries on Living, Second Series*, p. 40.

"The image is . . . the future." From the tape of the talk at Saanen on July 12, 1979.

"When you understand . . . an image." From the tape of the talk at Saanen on July 26, 1983.

"Any form . . . beauty of relationship." From the sixth conversation with Dr. Bohm and Dr. Shainberg in *The Wholeness of Life*.

THINKING
From the talk at Saanen on July 10, 1985, in *The Last Talks at Saanen, 1985*.

HURT
From the tape of the talk at Brockwood Park on August 31, 1976.

ATTENTION
From the tape of the talk at Ojai on May 7, 1981.

VULNERABILITY
"When reason . . . flame of love." From the talk at Ommen on August 10, 1937, in *The Collected Works*.

"As this is . . . attention to it." From the recording of the dialogue at Saanen on August 2, 1967.

"Do you see . . . around yourself." From *Commentaries on Living, Second Series*, p. 90.

"The essence of . . . any formula." Extracts from the dialogue at Saanen on August 8, 1965, in *The Collected Works*.

PERCEPTION
"What does perception . . . the observed." Extracts from *The Wholeness of Life*, pp. 237–38.

"All the sensory impressions . . . is disorder." Extracts from *Tradition and Revolution*, pp. 114–16.

"There is a totally . . . thought and time." From the tape of the talk at Saanen on July 16, 1981.

"Is there a perception . . . there is danger." Extracts from *Krishnamurti in India, 1970–71*, p. 65.

"What matters . . . what truth is." Extracts from the talk at Bombay on December 23, 1959, in *The Collected Works*.

"If thought continues . . . listening to you." From *Krishnamurti in India, 1970–71*, p. 52.

"Perception implies . . . that is beauty." Extracts from *Tradition and Revolution*, pp. 47, 49.

"There can be perception . . . brain is quiet." From the tape of the second conversation with Dr. Bohm at Brockwood Park on June 20, 1983.

INSIGHT

"What is insight . . . hurt is dissolved." Extracts from the tape of the talk at Brockwood Park on August 30, 1979.

"What is insight . . . that carry memory." Extracts from the tape of the talk at Brockwood Park on August 31, 1980.

"When you have . . . comes intelligence." From the tape of the talk at Saanen on July 16, 1974.

"This constant insight . . . in conclusion." Extracts from the tape of the talk at Saanen on July 18, 1972.

"Insight is . . . caught in time." From the tape of the talk at Brockwood Park on September 18, 1979.

PASSION

"When you fall . . . cannot go beyond." Extracts from the talk at Saanen on August 5, 1962, in *The Collected Works*.

"When there is no . . . passion." From the tape of the talk at Brockwood Park on September 4, 1973.

"For most of us . . . must have passion." Extracts from the talk at Madras on January 26, 1964, in *The Collected Works*.

"Remaining with suffering . . . beauty can exist." Extracts from the conversation on February 22, 1974, with Dr. A. W. Anderson.

"A mind that . . . is absent." From the talk at Madras on November 16, 1958, in *The Collected Works*.

"The perception . . . measureless." From the talk at Bombay on November 26, 1958, in *The Collected Works*.

"One has . . . sorrow." From the talk on July 24, 1985, in *The Last Talks at Saanen, 1985*.

ACTION

From the tape of the talk at Ojai on April 13, 1976.

LEARNING

"When do you . . . I am learning." From the talk in London on April 26, 1965, in *The Collected Works*.

"Knowledge is . . . the past." Extracts from the talk in New Delhi on November 30, 1967, in *The Collected Works*.

"Now we are . . . perception-action." Extracts from the tape of the talk at Saanen on July 14, 1981.

"When you are . . . to an end." Extracts from the talk in New Delhi on October 28, 1964, in *The Collected Works*.

MEDITATION

From the talk in London on June 26, 1955, in *The Collected Works*.

PART III: ACTION THROUGH INACTION

Observing

From the tape of the talk at Saanen on July 13, 1976.

Staying with "What Is"

"I want to see . . . takes place then?" Extracts from *Exploration into Insight*, pp. 136, 137, 138.

"Let's first remain . . . totally unreal." Extracts from the seminar meeting at Brockwood Park on September 17, 1978.

"Look, there is . . . comes clarity." Extracts from the tape of the dialogue at Saanen on August 4, 1968.

"Can the mind . . . do it, please." Extracts from the tape of the dialogue at Saanen on August 1, 1974.

"The man who . . . no marks." From *Tradition and Revolution*, p. 29.

"What is important . . . 'what is.' " From the tape of the talk at Brockwood Park on August 29, 1985.

"Try remaining . . . knows no summer." Extracts from *Commentaries on Living, Third Series*, p. 196.

"If you remain . . . flame of passion." From the tape of the talk on December 13, 1970, at New Delhi.

"Remain with . . . escape from it." From the tape of the talk at San Francisco on March 17, 1973.

"You have done . . . flower blooming." Extracts from the tape of the question-and-answer meeting at Saanen on July 23, 1985.

"Usually in our relationship . . . *should* be." Extracts from the tape of the seminar meeting at Brockwood Park on September 17, 1978.

"To stay with fear . . . just look at it." From the tape of the question-and-answer meeting at Ojai on May 19, 1983.

"When you begin . . . including God." Extracts from the tape of the talk at Saanen on July 17, 1985.

"Is it possible . . . my observation?" From the tape of the seminar at New Delhi on November 5, 1981.

"When you are . . . of freedom." Extracts from the tape of the talk at New York on April 10, 1983.

"There is an ending . . . insensitive to it." From the tape of the talk at Bombay on February 7, 1981.

Asking but Not Answering Fundamental Questions

"We are used to . . . an ecstasy, a bliss." Extracts from the talk at Bombay on March 13, 1955, in *The Collected Works*.

"You have to . . . seeking an answer." From the talk at Varanasi on January 3, 1962, in *The Collected Works*.

"I feel it is . . . different takes place." Extracts from the talk at Ojai on July 7, 1955, in *The Collected Works*.

"We know the mind . . . comes into being." Extracts from the talk at Madras on February 2, 1952, in *The Collected Works*.

"It is only the mind . . . extraordinarily sensitive." From the talk at Madras on December 3, 1961, in *The Collected Works*.

"To fundamental questions . . . brings about understanding." From the talk at Ojai on July 6, 1955, in *The Collected Works*.

"There is no . . . of the problem." From the talk at Bombay on December 17, 1958, in *The Collected Works*.

"There is a . . . observe, and listen." From the talk at Madras on December 13, 1961, in *The Collected Works*.

"If you put . . . your conditioning." From the talk at Varanasi on January 14, 1962, in *The Collected Works*.

"Is it possible . . . see what happens." From the tape of the talk at Brockwood Park on August 24, 1985.

The Beauty of Not Knowing

"Being afraid of death . . . therefore of meditation." Extracts from the talk at Ojai on May 29, 1960, in *The Collected Works*.

"If you are asked . . . tremendous revolution." Extracts from the talk at Ojai on July 21, 1955, in *The Collected Works*.

"Only the mind . . . come into being." Extracts from the talk at Stockholm on May 22, 1956, in *The Collected Works*.

"What is love . . . love?" From the tape of the dialogue at Rishi Valley on December 7, 1985.

"The mind that lives . . . is the prison." Extracts from *Tradition and Revolution*, p. 97.

"I am not against . . . I am learning." From the talk in London on April 26, 1965, in *The Collected Works*.

"Now can the mind . . . which is death?" From the talk at Madras on December 12, 1954, in *The Collected Works*.

"Can the mind free . . . search for security." From the talk at Stockholm on May 15, 1956, in *The Collected Works*.

On Issues Often Discussed

"The fear of death . . . the unknown." From the talk at Poona on October 3, 1948, in *The Collected Works*.

"To go inward . . . has no limit." From the tape of the talk in London on March 16, 1969.

"When I understand . . . comes love." From the talk at Poona on September 14, 1948, in *The Collected Works*.

"The mind . . . going to happen." From the talk in Paris on September 17, 1961, in *The Collected Works*.

"When the whole . . . the known." From the tape of the talk at Saanen on August 5, 1970.

"It is only when . . . there is God." From the talk at Bombay on March 4, 1953, in *The Collected Works*.

"The ending of . . . goodness." From the tape of the talk at Brockwood Park on June 23, 1982.

"In becoming something . . . complete security." From the tape of the talk at Saanen on July 17, 1975.

"To be free of . . . active present." From the tape of the talk at New York on October 8, 1968.

"To be willing . . . supreme intelligence." From the tape of the 1965 conversation with David Bohm in London.

"Freedom from . . . field of the known." From the tape of the talk at Madras on January 2, 1979.

"What takes place . . . beauty of it." From the tape of the talk at Saanen on August 3, 1973.

"If I love my wife . . . different quality." From the tape of the talk in London on March 23, 1969.

"You can know . . . meet the unknown." From the talk at Ommen on August 4, 1938, in *The Collected Works*.

Books by J. Krishnamurti

Can Humanity Change?: J. Krishnamurti in Dialogue with Buddhists

Many have considered Buddhism to be the religion closest in spirit to J. Krishnamurti's spiritual teaching—even though the great teacher was famous for urging students to seek truth outside organized religion. This record of a historic encounter between Krishnamurti and a group of Buddhist scholars provides a unique opportunity to see what the great teacher had to say himself about Buddhist teachings.

Facing a World in Crisis: What Life Teaches Us in Challenging Times

Facing a World in Crisis presents a selection of talks that Krishnamurti gave on how to live and respond to troubling and uncertain times. His message of personal responsibility and the importance of connecting with the broader world is presented in a nonsectarian and nonpolitical way. Direct and ultimately life-affirming, this book will resonate with readers looking for a new way to understand and find hope in challenging times.

Freedom, Love, and Action

In *Freedom, Love, and Action*, Krishnamurti points to a state of total awareness beyond mental processes. With his characteristic engaging, candid approach, Krishnamurti discusses such topics as the importance of setting the mind free from its own conditioning; the possibility of finding enlightenment in everyday activities; the inseparability of freedom, love, and action; and why it is best to love without attachment.

Inward Revolution: Bringing about Radical Change in the World

Here, J. Krishnamurti inquires with the reader into how remembering and dwelling on past events, both pleasurable and painful, give us a false sense of continuity, causing us to suffer. His instruction is to be attentive and clear in our perceptions and to meet the challenges of life directly in each new moment.

Meditations

This classic collection of brief excerpts from Krishnamurti's books and talks presents the essence of his teaching on meditation—a state of attention, beyond thought, that brings total freedom from authority and ambition, fears and separateness.

Talks with American Students

In 1968—a time when young Americans were intensely questioning the values of their society—Krishnamurti gave a series of talks to college students in the United States and Puerto Rico, exploring the true meaning of freedom and rebellion. Collected in this book, these lectures are perhaps even more compelling today, when both adults and young people are searching for the key to genuine change in our world.

This Light in Oneself: True Meditation

These selections present the core of Krishnamurti's teaching on meditation, taken from discussions with small groups, as well as from public talks to large audiences. His main theme is the essential need to look inward, to know ourselves, in order really to understand our own—and the world's—conflicts. He offers timeless insights into the source of true freedom and wisdom.

Where Can Peace Be Found?

Krishnamurti here teaches that the war and destruction human beings wreak on each other and the environment are caused by our misplaced attachment to a sense of self and individuality that leads to aggression, competition, greed, and conflict. When we recognize that our consciousness is not individual but common to all humans, we can work together in a spirit of cooperation and compassion. He also shows that taking personal responsibility for our actions and reactions—in our relationships and in our lives—is the necessary first step toward a global view.